Pentru

GIVING GOD THE GLORY: THE LIFE OF PETER SLOBODIAN

Founder of Baptist International Evangelistic Ministries

Compiled and edited by Sam Slobodian and Rick Barry

The story of how the Lord used one man from an obscure background to touch souls on multiple continents with the Gospel of Jesus Christ

Trăiește-ți viața în asultare de Cuvîntul Lui Dumnezeu și vei fi un exemplu pentru alții, cum au fost înaintașii noștri

Cu drag fam Simatic

Giving God the Glory: The Life of Peter Slobodian
The story of how the Lord used one man from an obscure background to touch souls on multiple continents with the Gospel of Jesus Christ.

Compiled and edited by Sam Slobodian and Rick Barry

Printed by:
Nystrom Publishing Company, Inc.
9100 Cottonwood Lane N
Maple Grove, MN 55369

Printed in the United States of America

ISBN: 978-0-615-49023-6

Dedicated to Mary Slobodian,
Peter's wife and faithful
helper throughout his lifelong
ministry in the Gospel.

ACKNOWLEDGEMENTS

Much of the material in these pages comes directly from Dr. Peter Slobodian, who left written accounts of many vivid memories and events from his own life and from those of his family members. However, other individuals also provided valuable assistance with details, photographs, supplementary explanations, and the editing of this biography. In this regard, the compilers particularly wish to thank Peter Slobodian's wife Mary (Maria) Slobodian, Ann Slobodian Shrader, Debbie Slobodian Rea, Gloria B. Durik Lenchuk, Susana Slobodian Georgescu, Marta Slobodian, and Sarah Slobodian Crouch. Each of them has provided help, without which this volume would not have been possible. Sincere appreciation also goes to the dedicated staff of Nystrom Publishing, whose suggestions and expertise in the formatting and production of this book were invaluable. Thanks to one and all for your personal contributions!

Foreword

One of the most memorable experiences I was privileged to share with my father, Peter Slobodian, was when, late in his life, we had the opportunity to travel together to the village in Western Ukraine where he was born. All my life I had heard countless stories about his early childhood in that village. They were such fascinating events that we family members didn't mind when they were repeated over and over again. One of those details that my father restated from time to time was that the Slobodian home was "the very first house in the village."

As the date for our visit to the small village of Hlibiv approached, both of us grew ever more excited about this chance to visit the scenes of his childhood years. Although I had never been there, I already possessed a vivid mental picture of Hlibiv through the stories I heard. This picture was painted yet again by my father, who rehearsed his stories once more as we rode together through the Ukrainian countryside. Once more, I heard how he had lived in "the very first house" as you drew near to the village.

As our car approached Hlibiv, we came within view of an impressive brick structure that marked the village limits. We stopped the car to photograph ourselves with this sign, then proceeded into the village. I was a little surprised when we didn't stop at the first house, but instead continued down the road. I didn't ask why we didn't stop immediately at that first house. I was certain we would go back, though. After all, it was like Dad, the master storyteller, to save the best for last. Besides, as Dad stopped to speak to every soul on the road we already felt a mounting sense of anticipation. As we progressed through frequent conversations, we finally reached the village center. There stood the Greek Catholic church, the village hall, the police station, the post office, and the school. Even after so many years, the street on which we stood was still the only street in town. All the homes and buildings in Hlibiv lined this one solitary street. It was a typical Ukrainian village, just like countless others I had seen. Although to us this one was special—*very* special—there wasn't anything remarkable that anyone else could have detected.

Now that we had seen the main buildings, I assumed our path would now take us back to that first house, the Slobodian ancestral home from long ago. However, we continued forward, farther along that single street, which grew narrower and narrower. When we reached the point where the road ended, my father stopped and pointed to the last house on the left and said, "That is our neighbor's house. Our house is no longer there. It was one house farther."

As I looked at the place where the house had been, I realized that it never could have been "the first house" in the village. It had been, in fact, the last house! Stunned and puzzled at the same time, I wondered how this could be. Anyone entering Hlibiv and asking for directions to the Slobodian home would be told, "Follow this road to the *last* house on the left." How could my father repeatedly describe the old Slobodian home as the very first house when, clearly, it was the very last one? Questions raced through my mind. I didn't voice them aloud, but of course that didn't stop me from thinking, "Dad was wrong on this one."

As we stood on the very ground where my father grew up, he became intense and animated as he described the scene just past the location of his house. As he pointed out the pasture where he tended the family cow, the river where he loved to fish, the fields where he had worked, the forest where he and his father hunted, I realized that those places outside of Hlibiv were the places where he spent most of his childhood. Those fields, the river, and the forest formed the center of his boyhood world, the fulcrum from which everything swung. From that perspective, as one looked toward town, his house *was the first house in the village!*

The Slobodian home was likely the poorest house of the village as well. The family's poverty would explain why, of all the houses on the street, this particular one hadn't survived the passing of time. As I gained further appreciation for the obscurity of the location, the poverty of such roots, and the unlikelihood that one who would launch a world-wide ministry could come from such a place, yet another perspective came to mind concerning the grace of God and this house. From the perspective of God—in whose presence Peter Slobodian now resides—was this not also the first house? When God directed His grace unbounded and blessings eternal to that area of Ukraine, upon which house did His presence shine the brightest? Without question, it was on that house, the poorest of them all.

This book is the story of how God blessed that house and that family from the village of Hlibiv in a particularly extraordinary way. For it was, indeed, the hand of God that took that boy and fashioned him into a choice vessel through which countless men, women, and children in far-ranging corners of the globe heard the Gospel.

"Yes, Dad, you were never more right; that house indeed was the first house from among them all."

—*Sam Slobodian*

GIVING GOD THE GLORY:
THE LIFE OF PETER SLOBODIAN

Introduction

The founder of Baptist International Evangelistic Ministries, Dr. Peter Slobodian, came from a fascinating background. During Peter's lifetime, he lived on three continents and automatically grew up speaking several different languages due simply to his surroundings. Later in life, he formally studied yet other tongues, plus theology, for the purpose of preaching the Gospel and planting churches. Academically, Peter earned several advanced degrees, including Master of Theology, Doctor of Theology, and Doctor of Philosophy. However, he never forgot his humble beginnings, and he never let academic achievement outshine his fervor for preaching salvation from sin through Jesus Christ.

What kind of background is required for a person to become a successful missionary-evangelist? The Apostle Paul was certainly a steadfast evangelist in the Roman Empire, and he grew up learning the Scriptures at the feet of a scholar named Gamaliel (Acts 22:3). But other New Testament evangelists arose from less studious backgrounds. Peter, James, and John had been fishermen. Matthew had labored as a civil-service employee—a tax collector. So a family tree that includes fame, fortune, or scholarship has certainly never been a prerequisite for an evangelist.

Even so, if one could invisibly return to the land of western Ukraine in the early twentieth century and visit the humble origins of Peter Slobodian, that experience might evoke wonder. In one obscure village, in a territory that had been occupied by one nation after another, God was moving to prepare yet another servant for a widespread preaching ministry that would touch lives around the globe. Peter's parents surely couldn't have expected such an outcome. Most likely, the newlyweds would have laughed in disbelief if someone had predicted the future that awaited their firstborn son. But God seems to take delight in plucking people from lowly beginnings and molding them to accomplish great things for Him. This was certainly the case with Peter Slobodian.

In publishing this biography, Baptist International Evangelistic Ministries does not seek to glorify its founder. Rather, the hope behind these pages is that the reader will praise and glorify God for this example of how He can raise up a choice servant, even from the most unlikely of backgrounds. An additional hope is that these pages will serve as encouragement to other present-day children of God. If any reader has ever been tempted to think, "I'm nobody special; I can't do much for God," then these pages will prove how wrong that conclusion is. After all, the examples from Scripture and the life of Peter Slobodian stand as solid evidence that one does not have to be "special" to accomplish special things for the Lord. After all, the Lord is the special One. He is ready to use any man or woman who sincerely loves Him and seeks to glorify His name.

Amen!

CHAPTER 1

Peter's Parents, Anton and Hanka

Peter Slobodian was born on July 9, 1923, in the village of Hlibiv (pronounced GLIB-uf; sometimes transliterated "Glibov" in English), which is situated in the Ternopil region of western Ukraine. At that time, the territory that has traditionally been called Ukraine was divided into four parts. One part was under the dominion of the Soviet Union; a second portion was under the control of Poland; a third part was under the sway of Romania, and the fourth part was governed by Czechoslovakia. Years earlier, when Peter Slobodian's parents were born in the 1800s, regions of western Ukraine had even been ruled by Austria. As a result, many citizens of Ukraine spoke Ukrainian, Russian, Polish, or even German.

Anton Slobodian, 1920s.

Peter's father was Anton Slobodian. By nationality Anton was Ukrainian, and by religion he was Greek Catholic. Peter's mother Hanka was Polish, and her family attended a Roman Catholic church. Both Anton and Hanka were born in the village of Hlibiv. Their houses were in the same neighborhood and stood close to one another. Although Anton Slobodian didn't admit it at the time, he had his eye on young Hanka for quite a while. In later years he would sometimes joke that he had "dated" Hanka for ten years. "For the first five years she didn't know that I was dating her and wanted to marry her," he would say. "But after those first five years, I did finally tell her that I wanted to marry her."

By nature, Anton Slobodian was a belligerent man. He enjoyed picking fights with men in the village for the sheer pleasure of fighting. People labeled him a *gooligan* ("hooligan"). Many feared him. If someone in Hlibiv had a "problem"—a grudge against another individual—that person could go to Anton Slobodian to arrange a solution. In other words, for a certain number of bottles of vodka as payment, Anton would go and settle the "problem." Of course, Anton's solutions usually involved his fists.

Hanka (right) with a friend in the 1920s.

Hanka, the woman who was to become Peter's mother, would urge Anton not to get involved in these disputes. But Anton wanted the vodka, and he enjoyed throwing his weight around, so he didn't listen. However, Anton's quarrelsome reputation among the local population would eventually lead to trouble.

Hanka's father was a prosperous farmer and businessman. Likewise, Anton's own father was a well-to-do farmer. Normally this combination of wealthy parents would result in a highly favorable situation for a young couple wanting to marry. After all, their prospects for nice wedding gifts and a sizeable inheritance would be excellent. They could look forward to living an abundant life. However, because of Anton's rough character, this wasn't to be.

When Anton and Hanka approached her father to ask for his blessing on their marriage, her father absolutely forbade Hanka from marrying Anton. He bluntly informed Hanka that she wasn't allowed to marry that worthless Slobodian hooligan. To add teeth to his edict, he threatened that she would lose her inheritance if she proceeded with the match against his wishes.

So the discouraged couple set off to talk with Anton's father. Perhaps he, at least, would give his blessing to the union. However, that hope also soon fizzled. Anton's father was outraged that any family would reject his son and accuse him of raising someone not worth marrying. Under those circumstances, Anton's father reciprocated with equal vehemence and an ultimatum of his own. He absolutely forbade Anton from marrying Hanka or he, too, would lose his inheritance!

What a predicament. Instead of blessings and hopes for a comfortable inheritance, the couple risked everything if they pursued their dreams of wedding. In the end, their decision was to defy both sets of parents. They agreed to relinquish their inheritances and to marry each other anyway. Their reasoning was simple: "We're not marrying for an inheritance. We're getting married because we love each other."

Both pairs of parents refused to back down from their threats. So when Anton and Hanka married without their families' approval, they lost the vast majority of their inheritances. As a result, the couple became poor. Instead of having their own fields to plant and till, they had to labor for other farmers. Anton also worked as a carpenter to supplement their income. Life was a struggle. (For the record, their parents on both sides did give them some land, but only as a technicality. In order to prevent villagers from gossiping that they gave their children absolutely nothing, the parents gave them tiny plots of ground. The plot from Hanka's father was subdivided further so that her two sisters each got a third. The result was that these tracts were so miniscule as to be insignificant for earning a living. Sadly, such behavior was especially typical of Hanka's father, who beat her severely several times while she was young, and for very little or no provocation.)

This was the scenario into which Peter Slobodian was born in 1923. However, in addition to being born to poverty-stricken parents, Peter entered the world with physical suffering. The midwife who attended Hanka when she went into labor was given to drinking alcohol. After she had delivered the baby, she hurried to Anton and exclaimed, "You have a boy! You should get out the vodka. Let's drink and be happy, because you now have a son!"

Anton was excited about becoming a papa, so he agreed with the midwife's suggestion. He opened a bottle of vodka, and the two began celebrating. Hanka, however, was physically exhausted after giving birth and fell into an extremely deep sleep. Peter began crying, as all newborns do, but there was no one to comfort or feed him. His mother couldn't respond, and Anton and the midwife promptly drank themselves into a stupor. Newborn Peter screamed and cried so hard that he developed a hernia.

That was the welcome that Peter Slobodian received the day he came into this world. There were no physicians available, and even with his mother's diligent nursing, the hernia required two years to heal.

As a child, Peter frequently asked his poor parents for a piece of bread to eat. The answer was usually, "We have no bread!"

Sometimes the Slobodians ate skim milk and borscht, which is soup made with beets. This was sour food, and Peter despised it as a child. As all children do, he preferred sweet foods, but sugar was an expensive commodity, which meant it rarely appeared in the Slobodian kitchen. In the fourteen years that Peter lived in Ukraine, he got a small taste of ice cream only a few times.

ANTON BECOMES AN ATHEIST

Despite the fact that Anton had lived a wild and wicked life, he began to feel emptiness in his heart. The partying and drinking and fighting no longer satisfied him. Somehow he arrived at the conclusion all by himself that what he was lacking was God. The more he thought about it, the more convinced he became that God is what he needed. So he began to ponder how he could get God on his side. Despite Anton's violent nature, he and Hanka took their children to church every Sunday. When the couple could afford them, he and Hanka also purchased icons of various saints to display in their home in hopes of winning God's favor.

One cold day in May, Anton had been working hard in a neighboring village and earned some money. On his way home, he began to imagine all the things he might possibly buy for those wages. As Anton plodded along, he hit upon an inspiring idea. He would save up his money and purchase a big statue of the Virgin Mary.

Coming from the background that he did, Anton's knowledge of God and religion in general were limited. However, based on his incomplete experience, he concluded that if he could buy a large, impressive statue of Mary the mother of Jesus, he would construct a special shrine for Mary to display in their home. They could then pray to that statue. In return, the statue would somehow bless them and improve their life spiritually and financially.

After Anton arrived home, he discussed the scheme with Hanka, and they both agreed to it. So the couple diligently saved their kopecks (similar to pennies) for a year or two until they thought they had enough. At last Anton hooked the horse to the wagon and traveled to the city of Ternopil, where he purchased a large, expensive statue of Mary.

When Anton arrived back in Hlibiv hauling a statue so large that it hung off his wagon, he and his cargo immediately became the main topic of conversation. When the neighbors saw the statue—and who was transporting it—many of them immediately wondered where the local trouble-maker had stolen it. Others immediately scurried off to tell the local priest what they had seen.

The priest was delighted. He declared, "I'm sure that Anton and Hanka bought this statue to present it to the church as a gift." So the following day, the priest went calling on Anton and Hanka to receive the statue on behalf of the church.

Anton had to shatter the priest's expectations. "I have felt emptiness in my life and cannot find satisfaction. I concluded that what I am lacking is religion. I think I need to get close to God, so I bought this Virgin Mary for myself, not for the church. I'm going to build a special place in my home, a shrine. I'll put her in it, and we will worship her. Then perhaps Mary will bless me and improve the condition of my pitiful life. Maybe then I will find satisfaction."

So the priest departed, deeply disappointed because he didn't get the statue.

All this happened the first week of May, and the weather was still quite cold. Anton carried some boards into the house and proceeded to fashion a shrine for his new prized possession. That shrine was supposed to be the centerpiece of their humble home, which reflected their poverty with its dirt floors and thatched grass roof. Until the shrine was ready, he decided to display the statue of Mary near the window. That house had a large window, and right outside the window grew a tree. Birds nested in the tree, and that day the birds were flitting from branch to branch, which thoroughly captivated the Slobodians' cat. Peering through the glass, she watched the birds from inside. When one bird glided especially close to the window, the cat leaped to pounce on it. Instead of catching its prey, however, the cat banged into the windowpane, and then tumbled backward in surprise. As the cat twisted in mid-air, attempting to land on its four paws, it collided with the statue, which toppled to the floor and shattered.

When Anton saw what had happened to his expensive statue of the Virgin Mary, he exploded in rage and frustration. All that money—wasted! However, when he finally calmed down, he decided that this accident was probably a good thing in disguise.

"I thought that statue was going to save me," he told Hanka. "But if she can't even protect herself from a cat, how in the world could she help us? Now I see that religion is nothing but a sham. The priests invented religion in order to keep people enslaved." He also told Hanka, "You can go to church if you want, but not me. I'm not going to church anymore."

So Anton Slobodian stopped attending church and declared himself an atheist.

Chapter 2
South America

Anton emigrates to Argentina

For the Slobodians, eking out a living in Hlibiv continued to prove difficult because they owned no real land to farm and couldn't earn sufficient money to buy a field. Mulling over his future, Anton grimly concluded that, unless something changed drastically, he would remain a pauper forever.

That thought was as depressing as it was motivating. If he were going to escape the clutches of poverty, Anton reasoned, then he would have to take some sort of drastic, radical action. About that time, a stranger arrived in the village. The newcomer was a recruiter looking for able-bodied men who would sail to Argentina to work there. "There's gold in the streets, just waiting for you to come and pick it up!" the recruiter told everyone.

Anton spent much time considering this opportunity. Sailing to South America would certainly be extreme, radical action. In the end, he and three other villagers concluded that they ought to go to Argentina. According to promises of abundant wealth and opportunities in Argentina, a healthy worker like Anton should quickly be able to earn enough money to return to Ukraine and buy a good-sized parcel of farmland.

During those economically depressed times in Ukraine, many did leave for other countries in search of a better living. Those who could afford the price of tickets sailed to the United States or Canada while others went to Australia. Those who couldn't afford those fares sailed to South America, where tickets were less costly.

Anton Slobodian in Chaco Province, probably 1931.

Excited that he had finally found a way to take his future into his own hands, Anton told Hanka of his decision. Hanka didn't accept it at first. After all, she wasn't the first wife from that area who heard such a plan. The familiar and sad pattern was that in almost every case, the departing husband never returned. Since some documents required her signature, she held out for a while. But Anton was far too determined and she couldn't withstand his forcefulness for long. So eventually Hanka consented, and they packed Anton's bags, and arranged for passage on a steamship.

When Anton arrived in Argentina, just as he had planned, he immediately searched for employment. However, this was the time of the Great Depression, even in Argentina. Despite the exhilarating rumors that Anton had heard in his homeland, now that he was in Argentina, he couldn't find a job. Alone and on foot, he searched everywhere for work as he plodded from city to city and from province to province.

However, if Anton was discouraged, at least he wasn't the only person in that pitiable plight. Countless other Eastern European men had traveled to Argentina for the same reason as Anton. These newcomers hailed from Poland, Bulgaria, Czechoslovakia, Byelorussia, and other Slavic countries. All of them had arrived in Argentina with high hopes of financial success. However, the reality of what they found in South America disappointed them. More than a few wished they could turn around and sail back to their native lands, but that wasn't possible: They didn't have enough money for return passage. Economically trapped, they had no choice but to remain in Latin America.

At times these wandering immigrants would band together. Finding others who spoke their language, they would discuss and debate the issues of the day and the problems they faced. During one such discussion in a market place, Anton—who remained a staunch Ukrainian patriot despite his homeland's economic woes—fired complaint after complaint at his new Polish acquaintances.

Anton concluded that the financial difficulties in Ukraine were the direct result of Poland's interference in Ukraine. In his home village of Hlibiv, he complained, even the language taught in school was Polish instead of Ukrainian.

"You Poles invaded Ukraine and snatched our land, but you don't know how to govern or how to solve our problems. Now Ukraine is in financial ruin! You're the reason I had to leave my country, leave my family, and come to Argentina. Now I'm suffering here, while my family is suffering in Ukraine."

Those Polish friends tried to defend themselves and their homeland. They countered, "Anton, we're in the exact same condition as you. You can see that we came to Argentina the same as you did. The Depression can't be blamed on Poland."

While this debate volleyed back and forth, a young Argentine man happened to pass by. He stopped and listened to the heated discussion, but he couldn't understand the tongue being spoken. He understood only Spanish. He stepped closer and caught the eye of a nearby man.

"What are all these men talking about so angrily?" he inquired in Spanish.

Understanding some Spanish, the Slav replied, "You see these men? They are from different Slavic nationalities. They are debating their problems."

However, in addition to "debating problems" Anton was just then loudly extolling the virtues of anything and everything Ukrainian. He praised Ukrainian culture, Ukrainian literature, Ukraine's poets... Anton's Ukrainian patriotism ran deep, and it wasn't uncommon. Many Ukrainians were known for these sentiments. In a book written in approximately that era, *Why They Behave Like Russians,* author John Fischer spotlighted this characteristic trait and likened Ukrainians to the Texans of America:

> The Ukrainians are the Texans of Russia. They believe they can fight, drink, ride, sing, and make love better than anybody else in the world, and if pressed will admit it. Their country too, was a borderland—that's what "Ukraine" means—and like Texas it was originally settled by outlaws, horse thieves, and land-hungry farmers, and people who hadn't made a go of it somewhere else. Some of these hard cases banded together, long ago.... They called themselves Cossacks, and they would have felt right at home in any Western movie. Even today the Ukrainians cherish a wistful tradition of horsemanship, although most of them would feel as uncomfortable in a saddle as any Dallas banker. They still like to wear knee-high boots and big, furry hats, made of gray or black Persian lamb, which are the local equivalent of the Stetson.
>
> The Ukrainians concede that their men and horses are bigger, their women a little prettier, than any others in Russia. They pride themselves on their freehanded hospitality, their easy friendliness, and they love to tell tall stories about Bogdan Khmelnitzky and Stepan Razin which sound

> remarkably like the legends of Sam Houston and Jesse James. They believe they won the war, with little help from the rest of Russia and none worth mentioning from the outside world. Nor is this conviction altogether unreasonable. One soldier out of every five in the Red Army was a Ukrainian, and their land was the great battlefield of the war; no other comparable area suffered anything like its devastation.…
>
> On all other people the Ukrainians look with a sort of kindly pity. They might have thought up for their own use the old Western rule of etiquette: "Never ask a man where he comes from. If he's a Texan, he'll tell you; if he's not, don't embarrass him." [1]

The young man pointed to Anton, who was the loudest and most vociferous in the group, and asked, "Who is that man, and what is he yelling about?"

"Evidently he is a Ukrainian patriot," came the reply. "He's telling everyone how great Ukraine is."

As it turned out, this young man observing Anton and the debaters was a student at a Bible school. Since classes were not in session, he, too, had needed a job. He had gone to a Bible Society and asked if they had any openings. They had no jobs, but they did stock him with Bibles and New Testaments and told him that he would receive a commission if he could sell them. When he heard that Anton was Ukrainian and a big patriot of that land, the student rummaged through his briefcase until he found a Ukrainian New Testament.

He stepped closer and looked Anton in the eye. "Are you Ukrainian?"

"Yes!" replied Anton proudly.

The young man's next question for Anton caught him entirely off guard: "Would you like to buy a New Testament in the Ukrainian language?"

---

1 John Fischer, *Why They Behave Like Russians* (New York: Harper & Brothers, 1947), 22–23

Anton later shared that his initial thoughts were, "Why would I want a New Testament? I don't care anything about religion. Those priests in Ukraine blinded our people with religion. This young fellow isn't dressed like a priest, but he is still peddling religion. I don't want anything to do with it!"

However, because Anton had just then been in the act of praising anything and everything Ukrainian, he suddenly found himself in a dilemma. As much as he wanted to reject that New Testament, he didn't want to turn down any sort of Ukrainian literature in front of the Poles, even if the literature was religious. After the impromptu speech he had just delivered, he didn't want to refuse a book in his own tongue.

"If I don't buy this book," he reasoned, "these Poles will laugh me to scorn for rejecting literature in my own language."

On the spot, Anton concocted a strategy that would enable him to avoid rejecting the Ukrainian New Testament but would also get him out of buying it.

"How much does it cost?" he asked, assuming he could scoff at the price.

"Only one peso."

One peso wasn't a large amount at all, so Anton realized he couldn't complain about the price. He needed a new strategy—and fast. Then inspiration struck: if he were to offer half price—just fifty centavos [basically 50 cents] for the book—surely the price would be too low, and this young fellow would stop bothering him.

He said to the student, "I can give you fifty centavos for the book, and not one centavo more."

"All right, you can have it for fifty centavos!" the young man agreed.

Now Anton had no way of backing out gracefully. He had to purchase the Ukrainian New Testament, and the young man continued on his way.

When Anton's companions saw that he really had purchased a New Testament, they immediately urged their nationalistic companion not to read it. Even though he hadn't wanted the book, their reaction sparked his curiosity.

"Why not? I paid fifty centavos for it. Why shouldn't I read it?"

The friends became more insistent, but Anton—who had never appreciated anyone telling him what he should or should not do—demanded an explanation.

"Give me one reason why I shouldn't read this book."

They begged him, "Don't read it! People who have read this book began to think funny in the head. They go insane! So be careful. Whatever you do, don't read that book, even if it is in Ukrainian."

As a result of these comments, Anton became unexpectedly fearful of reading his New Testament. After all, he didn't want to go crazy. But on the other hand, he didn't want to throw it away, either. After all, he had handed over real money in exchange for that little book. As a compromise—and to save face in front of his Polish companions—he simply stuffed it into his suitcase. That is where it remained for a long while.

Anton Slobodian in Argentina.

Anton continued plodding dusty roads in search of work. Time passed. Eventually, in 1933, about three years after his arrival in Argentina, the last of the pitifully few Argentine pesos he had managed to earn dwindled down to nothing. Because Anton was unable to find steady work, he had earned little money during the three years away from his family.

Now the predicament he found himself in was even graver than in Ukraine. Anton was too ashamed to beg for food and didn't eat for a whole day. The next day arrived and, again, he had nothing to eat and still couldn't find a job. By the third day without money, he was exhausted and famished.

"I'll probably die right here," he thought.

As he was walking, he lifted his eyes and spotted a tree a short distance away. It was a grassy spot, and the tree's branches provided a pleasant, shady place for the tired traveler. Anton decided to pause there and rest his road-weary feet awhile.

His situation was desperate: he was out of money and out of food. Even though he was positive he had nothing left to eat, he opened his suitcase and began to rummage through it. Perhaps he would find a forgotten crust of bread or some other morsel?

He found no food, but in that moment his eyes fell on the Ukrainian New Testament.

"I've never read the New Testament," he thought. "Why not do it now?"

However, even as Anton opened the little cover, a struggle began in his mind. On one hand, he felt strangely compelled to read this Book. But on the other hand he recalled the Poles who had so vehemently warned him against it. He remembered their adamant claims that people who had read this Book went insane.

Of course, he didn't want to lose his mind, but he still felt drawn to the beckoning pages before him. In the end, he devised what he considered a logical plan to make sure that he retained all of his proper mental faculties. He felt confident that, if it were true that this Book could drive a person mad, he would probably feel some sort of odd sensation coming over him while he was reading it. If that began to happen, he would immediately stop reading and would retain his sanity.

Anton flipped to the beginning and started reading the Gospel of Matthew. He read through the first chapter, then the second, and also the third. Then he paused for a minute. He turned his head to the left and then to the right. So far, everything seemed fine. He still felt totally normal.

"I still know who I am," he thought. "I don't feel any different." He concluded that his mind was working as well as ever and that he could continue reading. He read three or four more chapters. Again he paused and twisted his head to the left and to the right.

"I'm still thinking normally," he concluded with a shrug. So he continued reading his New Testament. He did the same after the next four chapters.

The story of Jesus' life impressed him very much. He learned how Jesus Christ was led to trial, where He was condemned to die. Anton understood that those who had condemned Christ to death held important positions in the Roman Empire. Also, he noticed that priests and high priests—whom he personally didn't admire—were among those who condemned Jesus. Lastly, Anton realized how Christ didn't suffer for sins of His own, but that He came to save sinners by dying for their sins.

Of course, not everything in the New Testament was totally new to him. Back in Ukraine Anton had already heard that there is a God. Anton also knew that God is holy, while he himself was a sinner, and he knew other bits and pieces of Bible stories. However, through this time of personally reading God's Word while sitting under a tree, a truth dawned on him that he had never heard before: that God loves sinners and that Christ came specifically to save sinners. For the first time he understood that Christ had also died for him, for Anton Slobodian's sins, and that fact gripped his heart like a vice.

Before long, Anton totally forgot about his plan to keep control of his thinking processes. He couldn't put the New Testament down and continued reading. Eventually Anton began to weep, and then he started to pray. There, all alone in the shade of a roadside tree, he asked God to forgive his sins and placed his faith in Jesus Christ as His personal Savior.

Anton's meeting with the railroad manager

At the precise time that Anton was weeping over his own sinful condition, the local railroad manager was trudging past the spot on his way home. He saw and heard Anton and stopped to talk with him. However, Anton didn't respond to his voice. The Ukrainian man simply continued his uncontrollable sobbing. The manager plodded home but couldn't stop thinking about this man who was weeping by the roadside. He told his wife what he had seen and heard and remarked that this was obviously a man in great distress. He told her the stranger had been holding some kind of book in his hands.

Coming to a decision, the manager determined that he would go back to that weeping man and check on him. He also asked his wife to prepare a meal.

"We'll give him some food," he told her. "Perhaps he is hungry."

The railroad manager hurried back to the place where Anton had been sitting and crying. This time, however, Anton was no longer weeping. To the contrary, he looked overjoyed.

The manager said, "When I was here the first time, you were sobbing so terribly that you didn't even hear me talking to you. You were holding a book in your hands. What kind of a book was that?"

By this time Anton had been in Argentina long enough that he could speak some basic Spanish. He replied, "It's a Ukrainian New Testament. I'm reading it for the first time in my life, and I discovered that Jesus Christ gave His life for sinners and that He died for my sins too. I prayed and asked for forgiveness of my sins. According to this Book, God forgave my sins, and I have become a child of God. I have a new nature! I've been born again. Now I don't need to cry anymore. I'm happy!"

The railroad manager was amazed and asked if Anton would like to eat.

"Yes! This is the third day that I've gone without food."

In the railroad manager's home, while Anton ate, the manager sat beside him and asked many questions about his family in Ukraine and about his motivation in coming to Argentina. After learning about Anton's desire to work and his inability to find a job, the manager wanted to help him. In fact, this manager had hired many employees for the railroad, and he said that he wished he could hire Anton too.

But, of course, he didn't want to fire someone else just so that Anton would have a job. So the manager decided to pen a personal letter of recommendation for Anton and instructed him to board the train and to hand-carry the letter to some of his colleagues in another town.

Anton said, "How can I go by train if I don't have money for a ticket?"

"Don't worry. I'll get that train ticket for you. After all, I'm the manager."

"What a wonderful man," Anton thought.

So Anton did board a train and was able to present the letter of recommendation to one of the railroad manager's friends. In fact, there was a job opening that very day, and Anton was hired on the spot. What an answer to prayer! Each day Anton worked for the railroad, and when his shift was over, he would go straight to his little room, where he continued to study his Ukrainian New Testament—and without any fear of going crazy.

The search for a Baptist church

Anton fell in love with his New Testament and continued reading it daily. He learned much from its pages. After a period of daily reading, he came to the conclusion that he should be baptized by immersion. That is what he saw portrayed in the Book. Of course, he had been sprinkled as an infant in a Greek Catholic church, but he now understood that that wasn't how God's Word described people being baptized. He was convinced that somewhere in Argentina there must be churches that believed and practiced in the manner described by his New Testament. He desperately wanted to find such a church. In fact, he dedicated every Saturday and Sunday to his search. He inquired of everyone with whom he came into contact. He would even knock on the doors of complete strangers in his attempt to locate a church.

Anton had a blunt way of posing his question. He would hold up his New Testament and ask, "Are you familiar with this Book?"

Some people would reply, "That's a Holy Book," or "Our priest has one."

Of course, he encountered people with widely differing religious affiliations. Some were Roman Catholic; others were Greek or Russian Orthodox. They would generally suggest that he visit their own churches, but Anton would reply, "I know all about those churches. I'm not looking for those. I'm looking for churches that practice what is written in this Book."

Anton Slobodian had become a Baptist by conviction without even knowing that term. Having read through the New Testament, he came to the conclusion that, even though he had been baptized by sprinkling in a Greek Catholic church, that experience wasn't a truly Biblical baptism. According to the Word of God, a proper baptism should be by immersion. It was very clear to Anton that in the New Testament, believers went "down into the water" to be baptized.

Anton searched for nearly an entire year before he happened across a Ukrainian family that seemed to understand his goal.

"There are people who baptize the way you describe," they told him. "In fact, back in our village in Ukraine there were people like that, and they had their own church. One time some of them visited us, and they sang some songs. We liked their singing, and they gave us one of their song books as a gift."

"Do you still have that song book?" he asked.

They did, so Anton asked, "May I see it?"

When he examined the hymnal, he noticed the address of a Bible society in the United States. Anton diligently copied that address. Back in his room, he wrote a letter to the Bible society and explained all about how he had received a Ukrainian New Testament, how he had put his trust in Jesus Christ, and how he learned that his baptism back in Ukraine hadn't been the proper kind of baptism.

He wrote, "Do you know of any church that baptizes the Bible way in Argentina? If so, please send me an address, so I can go to that church to be baptized."

When the Bible society answered, they sent Anton a gift: a Ukrainian Bible, both the New and Old Testaments. In joyful awe, Anton rejoiced over this unexpected treasure. In the letter that accompanied the gift, the Bible society said that they were, indeed, familiar with churches such as he described and explained that they are called "Baptist" churches. This was the first time Anton had heard such a name for a church. The letter included the addresses of a number of churches in Argentina, including a Ukrainian Baptist church in the capital city of Buenos Aires.

When Anton was eligible to receive vacation time from work, he purchased a train ticket and traveled to Buenos Aires, where he was baptized in a Ukrainian Baptist church. He returned to his place of employment and labored there for a few more years. However, being a farmer and also a carpenter, Anton decided to move to the province of Chaco, where farmers from many different nationalities were growing cotton. He discovered that those farmers had come from various countries with their whole families, and they were living very well. So he decided against returning to Ukraine and resolved to bring his whole family to Argentina.

CHAPTER 3

Peter on His Own

When Anton said good-bye to his family and boarded a ship for Argentina in 1930, he left his wife Hanka, his oldest son Peter, his daughter Olga, a second son named Nicolas, and another young daughter, Slavka. With her husband away, Hanka Slobodian had a genuine struggle to care and provide for four children in Hlibiv. She had to work extremely long hours every day. The family's meals were scanty and included potatoes instead of bread. The Slobodians owned one cow, so they had skim milk. They couldn't drink whole milk, because Hanka churned butter and sold it to buy kerosene, salt, and other needed items. A typical meal was borsch, which is a soup made from cabbage and beets. Peter despised sour borsch and craved sweet treats, but sugar was extremely expensive and thus a rare luxury.

Peter's mother Hanka (second from left) with a neighbor lady, her children, and Peter (second from the right) in Hlibiv, Ukraine, in 1930.

When young Peter started to work for big plantation owners, he had to toil for two and a half days to earn enough money to buy a kilogram (roughly two pounds) of sugar. Christmas and Easter provided two of the rare times each year when he tasted sweet bread or meat. As a result, hunger was a constant companion in Peter Slobodian's childhood.

The family's clothing was also pitiable. All summer Peter would walk barefoot every day, with only cheap shoes and slightly better clothing for going to church on Sundays.

Hanka Slobodian told her children, "We have to be a little better dressed for Sundays, to be among people and to enter the church. We might eat meager food, but nobody sees what we eat. We have to wear better clothes to go out in public."

Sometimes the family didn't have enough money to spare for clothing, so they simply had to do the best they could. In later life Peter remembered a time when he owned no boots, but winter was approaching. His mother told some relatives about his need, and they had a pair of high-heeled ladies' boots that they donated to him. Peter wasn't thrilled about learning to walk in those high heels, but he had to agree that it would be better than going barefoot in the snow. So he learned how to walk in them. Of course, all of the village boys laughed and poked fun at him for wearing women's boots.

The other boys would tease him with greetings like, "Hello, *Baba*," which means "old woman." But Peter had no other options. At least with the boots he didn't have to remain cooped up indoors; he could go to school and play outside in the snow. But when summer came, Peter encountered an unexpected problem: he had to relearn how to walk in low heels!

The summer when Peter was nine years old, he and his sister Olga went to labor in the fields of wealthy landowners. They toiled from morning until night and earned only forty kopecks—little more than pocket change. (At that time, fifty kopecks could buy approximately a pound of sugar.) So not only Hanka, but the children, too, began fending for themselves in Anton's absence.

During those years, Peter began "fending for himself" in other ways too—including avoiding school whenever possible. The school teachers in that region of Ukraine were poorly educated and certainly not high-caliber instructors. Parents who had some education could tutor their children at home and helped their offspring to understand what the teachers talked about to "fill in the gaps" in their children's education. In Peter's case, however, this didn't happen. Because Anton and Hanka themselves were not well educated, they couldn't help their son with schoolwork, which resulted in Peter being totally lost when it came to subjects like mathematics.

In Peter's mind, being good at math was only for students who somehow, mysteriously, became good at guessing the correct answers. The teacher hadn't explained the multiplication tables (or if she had, he missed that lesson), and his parents didn't know the multiplication tables either, so they couldn't help him. So whenever the teacher called Peter forward and asked him to solve a math problem, all he could do was to demonstrate in front of everyone that he wasn't a good "guesser" and to incur the wrath of the teacher. She made him hold out a hand and slapped it hard with a wooden ruler for not paying enough attention to know the answer. Because he failed to figure out "the secret of numbers," as he called it, he faced daily painful punishment at school and decided it was better to skip school than to face the whack of the schoolmarm's dreaded ruler. So that's what he did. However, when the school teacher told Hanka about Peter's skipping, his mother set out to find him. She caught up with him at the riverbank, where he was whiling away the day with his fishing line dangling into the water. Hanka grabbed him by the ear and marched her son through the village straight back to school. But, like a cat avoiding being dropped into a tub of water, as soon as he was inside the front door, Peter ducked and dashed out the back door! Without a doubt, if the citizens of Hlibiv could have heard a prediction that one of their own would one day become an internationally known scholar and preacher, not one of them would have pictured school-skipping Peter Slobodian in such a role.

Hanka and the Younger Children Emigrate

In 1936, six years after leaving Ukraine, Anton penned a special letter to his wife. He instructed her to prepare the necessary documents and to emigrate from Ukraine to Argentina with the children as soon as possible. After six long years in South America, he had finally earned enough money to wire Hanka the funds to buy steamship tickets for the entire family.

Passport photo taken of Hanka and the children without Peter.

With mixed joy and trepidation, Hanka began preparations for a move to the new world. However, when she went to arrange passage on a ship, her mounting excitement about the long-awaited reunion instantly deflated. The funds that Anton sent for his family's ocean voyage would have been sufficient one year earlier, but not anymore. Passengers who were eleven years of age or younger cost only half of an adult fare, and Anton had calculated precisely how much was needed for his family: one adult fare for Hanka, and four half fares for their four children, which equaled three adult tickets. But during the intervening years, the oldest son Peter had turned twelve. Now a ticket for him would cost another full adult fare—an amount that Hanka didn't have, even after selling her miniscule plot of ground to one of her sisters.

Peter Slobodian, 12 years old.

Hanka's decision was a heart-wrenching one. She told Peter, "You will have to stay in Ukraine a little longer. When we arrive in Argentina, your father and I will both be working hard. Before long, we should be able to earn enough money to buy your ticket, and we will send for you."

But as often happens, good intentions do not always pave the way to a happy reality. The departure of Hanka and the other children left Peter without his family, which was sad. But despite the gloominess of this situation, there was at least one gleaming beam of light for Peter: without Mother trying to force him, no one else cared whether he attended the village school. And he didn't. So multiplication tables—"the secret of numbers"—remained a mystery to him.

Preparation and traveling to Argentina

In 1936 Hanka and the three younger Slobodian children joined Anton. Two years later, in 1938, Anton and Hanka finally had enough money set aside to pay for Peter's passage, and they wired the funds to him. Because Poland governed that portion of western Ukraine at the time, the now fourteen-year-old Peter had to travel to an immigration office in Warsaw, Poland, to apply for travel documents for the trip.

For a day and a night Peter rode the train westward to Warsaw. Once there, he located the immigration office. However, getting the proper documents for international travel wasn't a speedy procedure. He ended up having to stay in Warsaw for several days. (Because of his young age and difficult situation, workers at the immigration office found him a place to sleep at night.) At last, when everything was in order, he began the return journey to Hlibiv.

On the way back, the train would halt at various stations along the way. One of those stops was in a sizeable Ukrainian city. As Peter gazed out the window of the train car, much to his surprise, he spotted a young man in a military uniform that he knew from his village.

"Ivan!" Peter shouted.

When Ivan saw who had called his name, he said, "Peter! What are you doing here?"

Peter explained how he had been in Warsaw arranging for his travel documents.

"Who is traveling with you?"

"Nobody. I'm alone."

Amazed, Ivan called over several soldier friends and asked Peter to tell them how old he was.

"Almost fourteen."

"Do you see this boy?" Ivan said to his buddies. "All alone, he traveled to Warsaw and arranged his immigration papers, and now—still alone—he is traveling back to his village. And he is only fourteen years old!"

When Peter reached Hlibiv, he had about two months to wait before he could board his ship. He used those days to visit all his friends and relatives in the surrounding villages and to tell everyone goodbye for what was likely to be forever.

During the two years that Peter had lived without his family, the villagers all came to know about his difficult circumstances. At first Peter lived with one grandfather. However, that man had remarried, and the step-grandmother didn't like having Peter to care for, so that arrangement didn't last long. So Peter moved three different times, each time going to live with a different uncle. The uncles, however, rather than viewing him as a family member to take care of, regarded Peter as a potential source of profit. They took advantage of the boy's plight and paid him a meager salary to perform taxing manual labor.

In addition, Peter rented out his services to other land owners to till their land for them. In this way, he stayed alive, and he had a room to sleep in, but now he had even less income than his poor parents had earned in the village. Of course, he couldn't spare money for luxuries, such as medical care. One day Peter got in a fight with another boy and ended up with a broken arm. He couldn't afford a doctor, so the arm wasn't set. As a result, when the bones began to mend, they did so improperly. At that point, one of the landowners Peter had worked for took pity on the boy and paid for a doctor to treat him. Because the bones hadn't been set, the doctor had to re-break the arm to set it. This time the arm healed correctly, but as a result, for the rest of his life, Peter's range of motion in one arm remained limited.

When the day for Peter to leave Hlibiv finally arrived, the news spread through the village. The others were glad that this boy's two lonely years without a family were now drawing to an end. As he walked down the street, at house after house people stepped outside and waved and repeated the call, "God bless you, our son!"

Peter once again boarded a train to Warsaw and made his way to the immigration office, where workers helped him with the final arrangements for the voyage to Argentina. Because Peter didn't have any money to spare, the staff in that office decided to help the boy to travel in the most economical way possible.

The office workers learned that, if Peter sailed first to France, he could board a ship that carried fifty percent cargo instead of just passengers, which would make his passage much cheaper. The advice sounded good. So Peter boarded a train in Warsaw bound for Gdansk, where he boarded a small vessel that carried him to France. In France he located the proper port and ship they had told him about, which was named the *Lipar.*

Aboard the *Lipar,* Peter soon learned why this ship was such an economical way to travel: because it carried so much cargo, the ship stopped in nearly every port. Altogether, Peter had to spend thirty days at sea to reach Buenos Aires, Argentina.

As a result of the frequent stops, Peter had opportunities to visit many cities that he never would have seen on a direct voyage. Whenever the ship tied up to a pier, the sailors allowed their passengers to disembark into the city. Because Peter was still a minor, he generally tagged along with some other family and went to admire the local sights. It was during this voyage that he saw and tasted his very first banana. At first he attempted to bite into it, skin and all, like an apple until someone took pity on him and demonstrated how to peel it. When at last he arrived in Buenos Aires, he didn't have any money left to buy a train ticket to Chaco Province, where his father, mother, Nicolas, and the sisters were living.

On an interesting side note, although Peter was unaware of it, his departure from Europe on the *Lipar* was quite timely. The family heard later that this was the last ship from France that could have carried Peter to the new world before World War II broke out. At the time, however, Peter was simply a young teenage boy on an adventure and enjoying his first glimpses of international horizons that he had scarcely imagined in Hlibiv.

Peter Slobodian was 14 years old before he saw his father again.

Once in Buenos Aires, because Peter was a minor, he had to remain in the immigration center. A guard would watch him all day, and another would keep an eye on his quarters during the night.

When Peter and Hanka received a telegram about their son's arrival, they needed more time to scrape together enough money to arrange for his train ticket. Days stretched into weeks before they could wire the proper amount. But at last Peter found himself on a train traveling the final twenty-four-hour leg of his journey to the city of Presidencia in Chaco Province of northern Argentina.

On the appointed day, Anton hitched a horse to his wagon and set out to meet Peter at the train station.

For the rest of Peter's life, he would recall the emotional moment when he peered through the glass of his train car and spotted one familiar face in the crowd—his father! His papa was a little older, but still easy for the boy to recognize. What a thrill! Peter hadn't seen his own father in eight years, and during those days of fending for himself, he had begun to wonder if he would ever see his family again. So there on the platform father and son shared an emotional reunion, complete with tears of joy. The plodding ride by horse and wagon out to the farm where Peter's family worked gave the two time to talk and to laugh and to catch up on each other's news.

Unfortunately, Anton didn't own a farm of his own. He and the family lived and worked on a cotton plantation. When the two reached the plantation, all the family rejoiced that—at long last— they were all under one roof for the first time in eight years.

When Saturday rolled around, all of the Slobodians spent their day off together. They talked a lot and simply enjoyed the pleasure of being reunited after such a long separation. On Sunday many of the Slobodians' friends and neighbors dropped by to congratulate them on the reunion. So Peter met all the family's local acquaintances. That was a wonderful, happy Sunday. As Peter enjoyed his family, he also got acquainted with their friends. His parents chatted much about farming in Argentina, and he saw how happy they were in the new life they had begun there.

But Monday, the beginning of the new work week, dawned soon enough. Because the harvest was still being gathered, the entire family trooped out to the fields to pull cotton. They worked the whole day. As Peter pulled cotton from the plants and stuffed it into a sack, he tried to imagine how much income a day of labor in Argentina would equal compared to a day of toil in Ukraine.

The Slobodians picking cotton.

"Father, what will we be able to buy with the money that we earn today?"

Anton replied that with the money the family earned that day they could buy a sack of 100 kilos of sugar, 100 kilos of potatoes, 100 kilos flour, and a little bit more.

"Father, since you have told me what we can buy, I see that Argentina is a country of abundance. It's not like in Ukraine, under the dominion of Poland and the Soviet Union. There I had to work two and half days to buy one kilogram of sugar."

After Peter had been in Argentina a few days, he asked his sisters and Nicolas what their arrival had been like two years earlier, about their own reunion with Father.

"You know, when we arrived, the first day was very happy and joyful. So was the second day. But on the third day, Mother started to scream at Father. She demanded to know why he had changed his religion. Why had he become a Baptist? Now they don't argue anymore, and we go to a Baptist church, but Mother insists on remaining Roman Catholic. So Father is a very good father, and Mother is a very good mother. But the two of them don't agree about religion."

CHAPTER 4

Growing Up in Argentina

One day Peter decided to ask his mother about changes he had noticed in his father. Although Anton was still obviously the same man who had raised Peter, it was also clear to the boy that something had altered inside of him.

Hanka replied, "You know, Peter, your papa is different from how I knew him in Ukraine. He does not smoke; he does not drink; he does not swear; and he does not use his fists the way he used to do in Ukraine. Most of the changes are good. He's such a good man now, and I like that. The only bad thing is that he has become a heretic from the church. I believe that he could live this new way of his and still be Greek Catholic like he used to be."

Anton Slobodian reading his Bible in Argentina.

As if in an afterthought Hanka added, "Your father reads the Bible every day, and he also prays during his Bible-reading time. He considers himself the head of the house and our example. So I advise you that, when Father is reading the Bible and praying, you should be respectful of that. Your brother Nicolas broke that rule one time, and he got a hard spanking for it. Since then Nicolas behaves, and you better be careful, too. If you don't behave, you'll get what you brother got!"

So Peter tried to respect his father's rules. Anton assigned to each child daily portions of the Bible to read and some verses to memorize by heart. At the end of each week the children had to give a report of their reading and recite the Bible verses that they had memorized.

When the cotton harvest drew to an end, a farmer hired Anton to work at his farm on a monthly basis. When that farmer learned that in Ukraine Peter had performed all sorts of farmer's work—plowing, sowing, cultivating, and other chores—he hired young Peter, too. When the next cotton harvest rolled around, the entire family joined in picking cotton again, and the farmer paid them based on how many kilograms of cotton they picked.

After Peter had been in Argentina long enough to learn some Spanish and to feel comfortable with life there, the Slobodian family needed some extra cash. So Peter volunteered to work for another farmer. When a sum of money turned up missing in that man's home, the farmer concluded that the guilty culprit must be his newest employee—Peter Slobodian. The farmer summoned the police, who showed up and promptly hauled Peter to jail without evidence and without a trial.

One night policemen unlocked Peter's cell and led him to a special room, where prisoners were interrogated about their crimes.

"Confess!" they shouted. "Admit you took the money."

When Peter maintained his innocence, they stripped him of all his clothing. Over and over they electrically shocked him. The brutal treatment continued until there wasn't a spot on Peter's body that they had not shocked with electricity.

"You can kill me, but I didn't steal any money," a frustrated Peter told them.

Whether they ever believed him or not, the policemen didn't say. However, after they finished torturing him, they gave his clothes back and released him. Perhaps the real culprit was discovered, but Peter never received an apology or any other word concerning his treatment in the jail.

Of course, there were schools in Argentina, just has there had been schools in Ukraine. However, because Peter had arrived not knowing Spanish, and because the family needed his help with manual labor, no one demanded that Peter immediately attend school. His brother Nicolas and the girls attended a regular Argentine school, but when Peter eventually returned to a classroom, he attended a trade school like many young men in his situation. When the admissions counselor asked whether he might be interested in studying business, he replied, "No, I don't know the secret of numbers." She explained that there was no secret, no magic formula, that all he had to do was to memorize the multiplication tables! At long last, Peter learned to unlock the mystery behind mathematics and really did take an interest in business.

Peter and a friend in Chaco Province.

The Slobodians get their own farm

Farming wasn't easy work. It was typically strenuous and occasionally backbreaking, but there was no choice. All of the Slobodians' ancestors had been farmers, so the family continued to work land for other farmers. Even though life now became more prosperous than in Ukraine, the family still didn't earn enough money to purchase their own farm. Because Peter liked farming, he assumed that he would be a farmer his whole life.

Anton teaching Nicolas how to shoot. Chaco Province.

"Father," he asked one day, "when will we be able to buy our own farm?"

Anton answered, "Well, it will take us some years. When we get enough money saved up, then we will buy our own farm."

"Isn't there any faster way to get a farm?"

"Yes, there is, but only if you're willing to work hard, even harder than we are working now."

Peter's enthusiasm immediately kindled. "Then let's do it! I'm ready to work even harder. So how can we get a farm?"

Anton explained, "We can get one by entering government property. It is forest land. We would occupy it. It would require an incredible amount of work to clear it—chopping down big trees, burning them, pulling stumps, clearing land to get clean soil..."

By this time Peter's enthusiasm was unquenchable. "Let's do it!"

Catching Peter's eagerness, Anton drove the wagon to the city, where he bought barbed wire. He then picked out a portion of government land, measured off one square kilometer, and then fenced it with that barbed wire. Even as Anton and Peter worked, they wondered if the government authorities would force them off this property. Government agents certainly had the authority and power to do it, if they so chose. But, hoping for the best, the Slobodians set to work chopping and burning massive trees. Such was their zeal that within a relatively short time they had cleared a good-sized parcel of land and planted cotton.

However, some neighbors who were native Argentineans didn't appreciate what the foreign newcomers were doing. They wanted to push the Ukrainians out. One day two men showed up and claimed that the government had sent them to expel the homesteaders.

Anton Slobodian clearing trees to build a family farm.

"What you're doing is illegal!" the men declared.

Anton looked them over and concluded that these two didn't look like government agents. He quickly realized that they were lying and trying to intimidate him. But Anton wasn't easily intimidated. Back in Ukraine, everybody in the village had been afraid of Anton Slobodian and called him a hooligan. Since then he had become a Christian and received a new nature, but the old nature was, to some degree, still inside him, too. Peter saw his father's eyes flash with anger.

"You see that road in front of you?" Anton told the men. "You'd better get down it as quick as you can—before I take care of you!"

The expression on Anton's face accompanied by the clenching of powerful fists told the men that this Ukrainian wasn't joking. So the imposter agents heeded Anton's warning. They set off down the road—and at a rapid pace! When they had run a good distance and felt confident that Anton couldn't catch them, they turned and shouted.

"Now you'll have to deal with other authorities. Men will come to drive you out of here!"

"They will come and will do the same thing you are doing," Anton shouted back. "They will run away just like you."

A few days later Peter watched as an official-looking automobile made its way up the road. When it crunched to a stop in the gravel, two unsmiling men stepped out. They marched up to Anton, and one of them said, "What did you say about us?"

Anton was puzzled. He had never laid eyes on these fellows before that moment. "I haven't said anything about you."

However, even as he was speaking, he realized that this pair looked like genuine government officials, so he guessed that the imposters must have gone to them and registered some kind of scathing accusations against the Slobodians.

"Oh, I think I know what you mean," Anton said. "A few days ago two local fellows came poking around here. They wanted us to vacate this property, so they put on a show and acted like they were government employees. I could tell that they were lying, so I ordered them out of here. But I see that you two are different. You two look like you really are with the government, so you I'm afraid of!"

Hearing that, the two strangers chuckled and actually became quite friendly. Glancing around, one of them said, "So what are you trying to do here?"

"You see, I have four children. I need to live, and I don't have enough money to buy a farm. My reason for being here is to start a farm."

"Do you know that it's illegal to do what you are doing?"

"I know that it's not the normal way to do things according to the law, but I'm trusting that something can be done to help my family and me."

The officials saw that this portion of forest had already been cleared of trees and that cotton was growing. Evicting Anton and his family now would not bring back the trees. "So you want to start your own farm?"

"Yes."

One of the government men pulled some documents from his briefcase and consulted a map to pinpoint the exact area where they stood. When they located the spot, they asked, "How many hectares do you need to farm?"

Anton explained that he had measured off one square kilometer and fenced it with barbed wire.

So they took a red pencil and marked the land on their documents exactly as Anton told them. They gave one copy to Anton and said, "There. The land is yours." At that time there were legal provisions for obtaining a sort of "squatters' rights" in such wilderness areas.

So Anton didn't have to pay—the land became his at no cost. The only thing the Slobodians had to invest was hard work. However, the soil on that new farm was exceptionally fertile because it was freshly reclaimed from the forest. As a result, the Slobodian farm became the best one in the vicinity. For a few years, the family worked fifty hectares as farm land, and they had fifty more hectares of forest. The government didn't even require them to pay taxes.

Hanka loved her "feathered friends" on the farm. Here she's feeding the Slobodians' geese and chickens. Life in Argentina was difficult, but still easier than it had been in Ukraine.

In time, the family's collection of livestock grew to about fifteen work horses, eight calves, a good number of pigs, various kinds of chickens, turkeys, geese, ducks, and doves. The Slobodians purchased much-needed farming tools, and life in Argentina became tremendously more prosperous than their old life in Ukraine. Next Anton decided to keep about 100 bee hives, so he was also able to sell honey. The profits from honey sales helped to pay for the younger children's schooling as well and other useful items.

The distance from the Slobodians' farm to Sáenz Peña, the second-largest city in the province of Chaco, was only ten kilometers. That meant big-city stores were not far when the Slobodians needed to buy something.

So, financially, life in Argentina took a significant upswing. On the other hand, Anton (who had joined a local Baptist church) was still the only member of the family who had been born again, and his family's spiritual condition weighed heavily on his heart. He continued to pray for them.

Working and studying in the capital, Buenos Aires

One day Peter had some free time, so he decided that he might as well read the Bible passage that Anton had assigned for the day. He was in the middle of his reading when Anton came indoors from the field and noticed his oldest boy reading the Bible. Anton walked over to Peter, placed a hand on his son's head and said, "My missionary!" But to Peter those words were just talk. They meant nothing important to him.

As Peter grew, he encountered young people from many Slavic backgrounds. Because they were not Christians any more than he was, Peter came to the conclusion that religion is just for old people, not for the younger generation like his. So Peter and his new acquaintances would go to dances. Those companions also coaxed him to try smoking. Peter did accept one cigarette, but he didn't enjoy it and decided that smoking wasn't for him.

Following his new companions' examples, Peter also tried drinking. However, he didn't care for the taste of liquor and never got drunk. Memories from his childhood exposure to the grief and damage caused by drunkenness kept Peter from going down that sorry path.

Eventually he went to work in the city, where he made more friends and adopted a totally worldly lifestyle. By this time he didn't attend church anymore, nor did he read the Bible or have any plans remotely similar to his father's wish for him to become a missionary.

Peter (left) and Nicolas (right) pose with a friend named Andres in Chaco, Argentina.

Knowing firsthand how much grueling labor farm work demanded, Peter set his sights on a different profession. He decided to enroll in a school to become a businessman. At first he began these studies near the family farm in Sáenz Peña. But later he transferred to a business school in the big capital city of Buenos Aires.

One time, when Peter returned from business school to the farm, Anton suggested to him, "Let's go to church."

"Oh, Father. Church is only for old people, not for the young."

Those words pierced Anton's heart like a dagger, but Peter had made up his mind. He was young, and he wanted to pursue whatever amusements he wished. He didn't consider going to church fun, and was adamant about not going. However, Peter couldn't imagine just how drastically his future was going to change.

In 1943 an American missionary named Constantine Lewshenia arrived in Argentina. This missionary had graduated from Moody Bible Institute in Chicago. Because his parents spoke Russian at home, he understood the Russian language. He had originally come to Argentina to study Spanish and was planning to use it to preach. However, upon arriving he was astonished to discover how many people from Slavic nationalities lived and worked in the industrial cities of Argentina. Since most of them spoke Russian, he decided to preach in Russian. Peter heard about the Russian-speaking American missionary, but paid no attention to the news. At least, not yet.

Constantine and Elizabeth Lewshenia, missionaries to Argentina.

The missionary leads Peter to Christ

Various preachers and evangelists visited the region where the Slobodians were living. Each one, of course, came ready to preach. But the fact that strangers bearing Bibles felt compelled to come to Chaco Province didn't make Peter feel the least bit compelled to listen. This Russian-speaking American didn't interest him any more than the other preachers.

However, several of Peter's friends attended the Russian-American's services and, much to Peter's surprise, they put their faith in Christ.

"Come and listen to this missionary from Chicago," they urged. "You'll be glad you did."

"I'm not interested in listening to him preach," Peter replied. "We're young. We should not be interested in religion. We have more important things to worry about—like how to improve life in Argentina, the economy, education, and political things."

The new believers replied, "Peter, you don't understand what it means to be saved and to become a child of God."

"I know a little bit about it," he countered. "My father is a Baptist. A few years ago I used to attend his church with him."

This revelation came as a shock to his friends. Nothing in Peter's worldly lifestyle had ever given them so much as a clue that he had ever attended church. "Your father is a Baptist?" they repeated in amazement.

"Yes, he's a Baptist."

"Why didn't you ever tell us your father is a Baptist?"

Peter was growing impatient with this whole irritating conversation. "Because I don't care about religion."

His reply was emphatic, so the friends didn't pressure him. They attended the church meetings without him.

A few months passed, and one Sunday Peter and a friend—basically his last close friend who had not become a churchgoer—were riding their bicycles to a dance hall. Along the way they encountered four other young people about their age. Could it be that they were heading to the dance as well?

The other riders braked their bicycles to a stop and invited the two young men to join them. It turned out that they were Christians, and they were pedaling to a church to hear the missionary.

"I'm not interested in listening to him," Peter answered bluntly.

But Peter's friend was curious. He decided to go and find out exactly what this missionary was telling everybody. He suggested a change in plans for the evening.

"All right," Peter finally relented. "We'll go. But if I don't like it, I'm leaving you at the church and heading to the dance by myself."

They reached the church early. The service hadn't begun. The missionary was there, and he was training some young people in singing four-part harmony. They had converted from various religions, including Roman Catholicism, Greek Catholicism, and Russian Orthodoxy. Now the American was teaching them songs that are sung in Baptist churches.

When Peter stepped inside this church, the scene that met his eyes somewhat astonished him. He had long since convinced himself that

God and religion were for elderly people, but a large number of males and females his own age were there rehearsing for the choir.

The missionary, Constantine Lewshenia, greeted Peter in Russian and asked, "Would you please tell me in which voice you sing?"

Peter thought, "Why are you asking me such a strange question?" But, smiling sarcastically, he answered, "I can sing in whichever kind of voice you like."

After hearing this spoken sample of Peter's voice, the missionary ignored the sarcasm and said, "You will sing bass."

The American's pleasant demeanor disarmed Peter. "I'll try," he agreed.

So Peter pretended to be singing, but mostly he was gawking around at old friends who had recently put their faith in Jesus Christ. They were now singing enthusiastically. He was amazed at how passionately these people his own age were singing about God and Jesus. It hadn't been so very long since those same friends and Peter had enjoyed worldly pursuits together. Before, they had sung sinful, worldly songs with him. Now, however, they were singing to the glory of God. Peter was baffled.

"How can they do this?" he wondered. It was almost as if they had been transformed into entirely different people with totally different interests, attitudes, and brains.

Suddenly the thought occurred to him that perhaps they had received something that he still didn't understand. Was that possible?

When it was time for the service to start, Peter's friend said, "Well, are you staying for the preaching, or going to the dance?"

"I'll stay and listen to the preaching," he replied.

Then Constantine Lewshenia preached on the words of Christ in John 8:12, "Then spake Jesus again unto them, saying, I am the light of the world: he that followeth me shall not walk in darkness, but shall have the light of life." Constantine was a young man, full of vigor and life. When he preached, Peter saw that he obviously believed what he was saying. But how could that be, if religion was only for old people?

"How can you be so young and believe in these things?" Peter wondered. Again, it occurred to him that perhaps this missionary possessed something that Peter couldn't comprehend.

At the end of this man's sermon, he gave an invitation saying, "Who wants to repent and accept Christ as personal Savior in order to have the light of eternal life? If you want to do that, raise your hand."

Peter observed quite a few hands going up.

Addressing those who raised their hands, Mr. Lewshenia invited them to walk to the front to show that they sincerely meant business with God. A mixed group of adults, young people, and even children slipped from their seats and walked toward the front of the church.

Peter felt embarrassed for those walking forward. "I would never do that!" he told himself. Privately he wondered if the American missionary was using some sort of mind control, or hypnosis, or other method of manipulating thoughts. Perhaps these other people were susceptible, Peter concluded, but he wasn't so gullible.

That night when Peter pedaled back to where he was staying in the city, his father was waiting for him outside the door. Anton had decided to drop by for a visit.

"Where have you been?" Anton wanted to know.

"I was at a church." Without going into great detail, Peter told how he and a friend had gone to hear the Russian-speaking missionary.

Tears glistened in Anton's eyes. "Peter, I have been praying constantly that you will become a believer. Now I see that you will."

Resentment surged inside the younger Slobodian. "You will never see me become a believer! If I ever do that, it won't be until I'm an old man."

This wasn't the reply Anton had expected or hoped for.

"But that missionary is going to hold one more evening service," Peter continued. "After that, he leaves to preach in some other province. I'm going to listen to him just one more time."

The reasons Peter had for wanting to go back had nothing with wanting to hear God's Word proclaimed. Rather, he was intrigued. Just how had that missionary persuaded so many people to turn their lives around 180 degrees? Like a spectator trying to glimpse the reality behind a magician's sleight-of-hand tricks, Peter wanted to figure out exactly how that American was getting hold of people's brains.

Anton, however, didn't concern himself with the reasons. He was just glad that his son would be listening to someone preach the Word of God. "Let's all go as a family," Anton suggested.

The Slobodian family on their way to church.

So that next evening Anton hitched the horse to the wagon and took his family to the service. During that service, Mr. Lewshenia preached on another passage spoken by Jesus Christ: "Peace I leave with you, my peace I give unto you: not as the world giveth, give I unto you. Let not your heart be troubled, neither let it be afraid" (John 14:27).

This time Peter paid less attention to his newly converted friends and more attention to the sermon. While listening to Constantine Lewshenia's preaching, Peter realized that he himself had been searching for some kind of peace in life, but had never found it. Bit by bit, Peter began to understand that he had never found that peace because he had been looking in all the wrong places. Suddenly the truth flashed into Peter's mind like a brilliant sunbeam: he could gain that peace when he repented of his sin and accepted Christ as his personal Savior!

At the conclusion of the service, when the missionary gave an invitation to come forward and accept Christ, Peter forgot all about his heated claim that his father would not live long enough to see him become a believer. Peter stepped into the aisle, made his way forward, and repented of his sins as he accepted Jesus Christ as Savior.

Back in his pew, Anton Slobodian's eyes brimmed with tears of happiness. With emotion beyond words, he praised God for working in his son's life. He also thanked the Lord for allowing him to see that day.

Just that abruptly, Peter's entire outlook on life changed. In the same way that his friends had become renewed from the inside out, Peter began to see life from a loftier perspective. He never gave his old lifestyle a second thought. He never went dancing and carousing with his unsaved friends again. He had planned on becoming a businessman, and just two weeks later he did receive his diploma from business school. Now, however, he felt that God was summoning him to a much more important business—the business of preaching the Gospel.

Peter was just two weeks away from graduating from business school when he accepted Christ.

CHAPTER 5

Peter's New Direction

Starting right after the evening of his spiritual rebirth, Peter began to read the Bible every day. Nobody had to assign him passages to read anymore. Overnight, the Bible became precious to him, and he

Peter's home church, Evangelical Baptist Temple, where he was saved and baptized. Bajo Hondo, Argentina.

sincerely wanted to understand everything written in it. Peter was
came active in the family's church, the *Templo*
to (Evangelical Baptist Temple).
onverts at that church desired to be baptized. The
ch had the opportunity to question all the candidates

concerning their salvation experience, about their understanding of baptism, and other matters related to the Bible. Twenty people were accepted for baptism, and Peter was one of them.

After being baptized and receiving church membership, Peter began riding his bicycle after each Sunday service to visit the farms of old friends. He wanted to tell each of them how he had become a new person. One time he arrived at a farm that had a dance party going full swing. When the party-goers saw Peter, they stopped the music. Peter recounted his testimony to all of the listeners, then invited them to the church before leaving.

Nicolas and Peter's sisters likewise put their faith in Jesus through the missionary's preaching. Lastly their mother Hanka was saved, too, so the whole family learned to love and trust the Lord.

In time Peter's new love for the Lord gave birth to another desire. "Father," he said, "I would like to enroll in a Bible school." But there was no Bible school anywhere in the district, so Peter didn't know what to do about this heartfelt desire.

However, when Constantine Lewshenia revisited the Slobodians' church a few months later, he brought some wonderful news. He announced that, with the assistance of other missionaries, a Russian-language Bible Institute had been organized not far away in Rosario, Argentina. It was called *Instituto Biblico Ruso* (Russian Bible Institute). At the time, this was the only Russian-language Bible institute in the world, and for Peter its location couldn't have been more providential.

Peter, Olga, and Nicolas Slobodian
in Chaco, Argentina.

This news immediately gripped Peter's heart. With tremendous joy he prayed that God would grant him the opportunity to study His Word at this new Bible institute. He wasted no time in applying and soon found himself doing the one thing that, until recently, he had never imagined himself doing: enthusiastically poring over the Scriptures.

The Russian Bible Institute was a three-year program and required six semesters of study. Initially Peter found his classes extremely difficult. He was even on the verge of dropping out of school and going back to business.[2] But when he wrote to his father commenting on how difficult the institute was, Anton wrote back with a Bible verse. This letter encouraged Peter.[3]

First year Russian Bible Institute students and faculty in 1944.

In that same moment, he recalled the day that his exhausted father had come in from the field and, seeing Peter reading the Bible, placed a hand on him and uttered, "My missionary!" At the time of the incident, his father's words had held no meaning for Peter. But now those words and that memory became precious to him. Re-energized, Peter changed his mind about quitting and determined that he would not go into business. Instead he would simply focus all his energy on studying.

---

2 After all, Russian was not his native language. At home Peter grew up speaking Ukrainian and Polish, and even though he could figure out Russian when it was spoken, being a student in a Russian school and performing all of his academic work in that tongue taxed his brain to the limit. Andres Prokopchuk taught a Russian grammar course at the Institute, and Peter immersed himself in the textbook during study hall after lunch. At his church there were some Russian folks who also helped by speaking the language with him.

3 The Bible verse his father sent as encouragement was Proverbs 6:4, "Give not sleep to thine eyes, nor slumber to thine eyelids."

The students who enrolled in that institute hailed from various provinces around Argentina, as well as from Paraguay, Uruguay, and Brazil. Peter's sister Olga enrolled at the same time as Peter. When they were in their senior year, their younger brother Nicolas also enrolled. But their youngest sister Slavka got married and didn't attend.

Anton and Hanka Slobodian in Argentina.

With three of their children away studying and a fourth one married, Anton and Hanka were left alone. Anton wrote to Peter, saying, "You all left us, so only the two of us are here now. We look like newlyweds, because we have no children."

Despite Peter's initial struggles with the course work, by the end of his third year he graduated with honors in 1946. In fact, the Institute graduated him *summa cum laude* as valedictorian of his graduating class. While there, one of his instructors, a man by the name of Filipchuk, insisted that his students pay attention even to tiny details of God's Word. Therefore he sometimes gave special quizzes in which the students had exactly one minute to find a particular phrase used in the Bible. Those exercises were demanding, but they served to help Peter pay attention even to small details and to recall them later when he needed a Bible passage, so Peter developed an

Peter's graduating class at the Russian Bible Institute.

excellent memory. (Many years later, when Peter was working on his doctorate degree at the California Graduate School of Theology, he traveled to the Holy Land as part of his studies. In Greece and Crete the students personally stood in historical sites where early church history took place. In Turkey they studied the seven churches of the Book of Revelation and then continued on to Israel, where they learned about Jerusalem and other geographical sites in Israel under a Jewish professor. At one point, when that professor was explaining details about the Valley of Megiddo, he posed a Bible question to the group. It wasn't an easy one. He told them that Solomon's seal had been found someplace where they had visited. He told the students that he would give a duplicate of Solomon's seal to the first person who could name the location where the seal had been found. Thanks to the memory for details Peter had developed back in his Russian Bible Institute years, he answered correctly on the spot, and the professor presented him with a facsimile of the original.)

After Peter graduated from Russian Bible Institute, his home church extended an invitation for him to become their pastor. As much as he appreciated the honor of being asked, Peter declined the offer. He had already decided that he didn't want to build on someone else's foundation. He wanted to begin a fresh work. So he started a new church in Sáenz Peña, about ten kilometers from the Slobodian family farm.

Peter and Maria

Being a preacher and traveling as he did in those South American countries to hold evangelistic meetings, Peter made the acquaintance of many young ladies in various churches. More than once, parents expressed hope that this preacher would take an interest in and marry their daughter. In fact, Peter began to notice a familiar pattern developing.

Typically, parents hunting for a stable, Christian husband for their daughter would casually bring up the subject of marriage and extol to him all the joys of marital bliss. Evidently they hoped that the single preacher would lament his unhappy state of bachelorhood and begin glancing around for the nearest candidate who might ease his miserable loneliness. However, rather than taking the bait, Peter demonstrated some "matchmaker" abilities of his own as he introduced some of his friends to these young ladies.

Peter often rode his bicycle to preach in evangelistic meetings.

As for himself, Peter had no immediate desires to marry. He would explain to such hopeful parents that he had decided not to marry and to continue his life and ministry as a bachelor. When he expressed his intentions in such blunt terms, they stopped pressuring him.

About a year after Peter's graduation his own mother Hanka asked, "Why aren't you married yet?"

"I've decided not to marry," Peter replied matter-of-factly.

His disappointed mother couldn't fathom such a decision, "Then what are you going to do? You'll make horses to be afraid!" [*Editor's note:* In rural Ukraine there have been a couple colloquial expressions that infer that a person has too much time on his hands and will get into mischief. Hanka's line about frightening horses was one, and "twisting cows' tails" was another. Both speak of being so idle that a person will waste time doing silly things.]

However, as months flowed passed, Peter's firm grip on bachelorhood began to weaken.

"Maybe it's finally time to look for a wife after all," he mused.

Shortly afterwards, while back at the Russian Bible Institute to take a course on music, he began to notice more seriously a young lady named Maria Vladimirovna Ermacovitch. She was also the niece of the Dean of Students, Andres Prokopchuk, and she lived with the Prokopchuks in exchange for doing household chores.[4] Although Maria, like Peter, came from a family with Slavic ancestry, she herself had been born in Campinas, Rio Grande do Sul, Brazil, and grew up near there in Santa Rosa. Both are small towns near the southern border of Brazil, not far from Argentina.

Mary Ermacovitch.

Almost instantly upon getting acquainted with Maria, Peter's remaining resolve to remain single crumbled

"What a beautiful Christian girl," he thought. "She's the one who's going to be my wife." .

The fact that Peter was about eight years older than Maria didn't stop him from paying particular attention to her. (Maria had arrived in Argentina in 1947, when she was fifteen, and lived in Rosario with the Prokopchuks for one year before she enrolled at the Russian Bible Institute at age sixteen.) When Peter felt that he had known Maria long enough, he developed a plan to propose to her. One day as he was chatting with her, he steered the conversation toward the subject of marriage. As the intention behind Peter's words gradually dawned

4 Peter graduated in 1946. Maria arrived in Argentina in 1947 and lived with the Prokopchuks in Rosario. She enrolled in 1948, the first year the Institute operated in Funes. (After several buildings were donated, the school relocated.) Mary graduated from the three-year-program in November 1950. The Prokopchuks often traveled to Buenos Aires in 1947 and took Mary along as they promoted the Institute in a church blessed with numerous young people. The three enjoyed fellowships in homes and also attended the church. It was on one of these trips that Peter and Mary met. They became friends and would join the other young people for activities. When Peter began reconsidering marriage, he corresponded with the administration of the Russian Bible Institute about possibly enrolling for a music course and perhaps a few additional classes. He never did that, but he did move to Funes, where he was involved in the local church and also helped/fellowshipped with the students and faculty at the Institute. There were special conferences, etc., so Funes became a hub of ministry opportunities, which opened additional doors of opportunity for Peter to consider.

on Maria, he popped the question. The flustered girl exclaimed, "What?" That exclamation was quickly followed by two more: "What? WHAT?!" .

Maria Ermacovitch
at age 16.

The conversation had abruptly taken an unforeseen direction.

Peter took courage and asked Mary, "Will you marry me?"

"Brother Peter, is this for real?"

"It is."

When she knew for sure that he wasn't joking, she replied, "I'll give an answer to your proposal tomorrow."

As can be imagined, Peter didn't sleep at all that night. Instead he thought about all the changes that might soon take place in his life.

The next day Maria gave him her answer. "Yes, I will marry you." Then she gave him two Bible verses, Song of Solomon 8:6–7: "Set me as a seal upon thine heart, as a seal upon thine arm: for love is strong as death; jealousy is cruel as the grave: the coals thereof are coals of fire, which hath a most vehement flame. Many waters cannot quench love, neither can the floods drown it: if a man would give all the substance of his house for love, it would utterly be contemned."

The Prokopchuks

In conclusion Maria added, "You have to know that my life is dedicated for the Lord!"

That was in 1949. Because Maria at age eighteen was eight years younger than Peter, was a student, and still had one year to go, the two decided to wait and marry after her graduation. Meanwhile Peter would continue his itinerant traveling and preaching. They never had an unchaperoned date. Typically, when Peter was in the area, he would visit the Prokopchuks' home to play checkers or similar table games with Maria. When he left on preaching trips, his letters were quite matter-of-fact and unromantic: "I traveled so many miles, I preached so many times in this church and that church. I love you." Maria and her Aunt Marta would pore over those letters trying to decide whether he really did love her!

However, even after Maria graduated in 1950, the couple encountered a dilemma. They learned that, because Maria was nineteen when

This photo was taken in Funes at the end of a revival series, which followed Maria's graduation. Notice that Peter and Maria are the only ones not looking at the camera.

she finished the three-year Bible institute, she was still considered a minor by Argentine law. She couldn't sign a marriage license and therefore couldn't marry. In order for her to get married before the age of twenty-one, her parents would have to sign for her, but Maria's parents weren't able to travel all the way from Brazil. So Peter and Maria's thrilling wedding plans screeched to a disappointing halt.

Not sure where to turn, Peter and Maria sought advice from a local judge in Funes. Might there be any legal loophole they could use in this situation?

"Yes, there is one other possibility," the judge informed them. But he didn't want to raise their hopes: this loophole wasn't a large one. "If a minor wants to marry, and her parents are not available to sign their consent, the only legal alternative is to receive a permit from a federal judge of Argentina."

That quest fell into the category of things easier said than done. Because it was late December and summertime (the seasons being reversed from those in North America), most of the Supreme Court justices were away on vacation. One solitary judge was working, they learned, but he was handling only critical matters that required immediate attention. Of course, marriage licenses weren't considered critical, so the couple's chances of obtaining an appointment with that federal judge seemed slim. But they decided to try anyway. They set off for the building where this one judge would be working. Once there, however, they couldn't even get through the door.

Peter and Maria pose for a photograph on the day of their civil wedding ceremony, January 5, 1951.

"You can't go in," the guards at the door stated. "Only people with official permission can enter."

Not giving up, though, Maria and Peter noticed a side door away from the main entrance. No guards stood at that entrance. Did they dare to hope it might be unlocked? The couple strolled casually along the sidewalk, then rushed to that side entrance. It opened!

"Halt!" shouted a guard who came rushing toward them.

But the couple had come this far in their quest, and they weren't going to stop now. They pounded down the hallway reading names at the doors as they sought the correct office. And suddenly—they found the right door! But then the pursuing guard caught up to them. Glowering, the man in uniform was ready to throw them out of the building.

Mary's bridal portrait, which the photographer displayed in his studio. She feared she would never get it back!

Just then, hearing the commotion in the corridor, the judge stepped out of his office. "What's going on here? What's the problem?"

The guard wanted to escort the couple out immediately, but the judge told him to wait while he listened to this couple who wanted to speak with him so urgently.

When the judge heard how Peter was a missionary and how Maria had just graduated from Bible institute and that they wanted to marry, he said, "It's not my responsibility to do this for you. However, I see that you are sincere and dedicated people. I'll write up a marriage permit for you."

Peter and Maria Slobodian married on January 6, 1951, in Funes, Argentina.

How they thanked the Lord that this man granted them their wish! So, with the proper document in hand, they headed back to their local courthouse and appeared at the office of the first judge they had consulted.

The judge studied their paperwork, and then eyed them with amazement. "I was positive that you wouldn't be able to get a permit. But now that you have it, I'll marry you."

So, in the end, the wedding that some people had considered impossible became possible. With prayer and diligent effort, Peter and Maria achieved their hoped-for goal. They married according to plan on January 6, 1951, in the city of Funes. (Note: Being south of the equator, Argentina's seasons are the reverse of those in North America. So January there occurs in summer, and that is the season in which they received the permit and married.)

Mary's family background

Like Peter, Maria Ermacovitch came from a Slavic background. But because most of their North American friends came to know her by the anglicized name of "Mary," from this point on, this account will refer to her as Mary rather than Maria.

Mary's grandparents and parents had emigrated from Minsk to Brazil, where she was born. By denomination her family had originally been Greek Orthodox. In fact, her grandfather once served as a *diak*, a leading figure who ranked in importance just below the priest.

Mary's maternal grandparents and family, Mikhail and Maria (Michalowski) Stragevitch.

Numerous immigrants from diverse lands lived in the Ermacovitches' colony in Brazil. Shortly after the turn of the twentieth century, Brazil launched a program to lure resourceful and hardworking Europeans to come and settle in new colonies. (Mary's mother and grandparents joined about thirty other families from Minsk who sailed aboard one ship in 1912, the same year the *Titanic* sank.) The Brazilian government offered to pay the ocean passage for settlers from Byelorussia, Poland, Portugal, Italy, and other lands. Among these emigrants were a good number of Germans, some of which were Baptists. Mary's mother Natalia became close friends with

German young people in school. By constantly associating with Germans, she learned to understand and speak the German language. When these German friends invited her to their Baptist church, Natalia accepted the invitation. She attentively listened to the pastor, understood the Gospel, and placed her faith in Jesus Christ. Instead of returning to her father's Greek Orthodox church, Natalia began attending the Baptist church and became quite active in it.

Mary Slobodian with sisters Olga and Anna.

However, when the Greek Orthodox priest and all his parishioners learned that Natalia had become a Baptist, they criticized her father, the *diak*. They would shake their heads and say, "How is it that you hold such a high position in our church, but your daughter goes to the church of those German heretics? You should stop her from going there. Bring her back to the Orthodox church!"

So Natalia's father—Mary's grandfather—resolved to force his daughter back into the ranks of Greek Orthodoxy. He flatly ordered her not to attend the "heretical" German church. But Sunday arrived, and she didn't show up at the Orthodox service. Instead, her footsteps led her once again to the German Baptist church.

When Natalia returned home, her father was irate that she had disobeyed his command. "If you go back to those Baptists next Sunday, I'll come in there for you with a stick, and I'll drag you out of their church building. I'll spank you in front of all of them, showing what a disgrace you are for me. Then I'll bodily drag you to the Orthodox church!"

Seven days later, Sunday dawned, and the *diak* was confident that his daughter would not dare return to the Baptists. But when it was the hour for the service in the Orthodox church to begin, he began scanning faces for Natalia. He didn't see her. He asked his wife where Natalia was, and she replied that she didn't know either. The truth struck him like a thunderclap.

"So! She has disobeyed again. I'll march over there and do exactly what I told her I would do!"

The *diak* found a good, sturdy stick and headed down the road to the German Baptist church. When he arrived, he stood in the doorway and clutched the stick behind his back while his eyes roved back and forth, searching the auditorium for Natalia. He didn't spot her among the congregants. Next he gazed at those on the platform and finally found Natalia singing in the choir. Now what should he do? Angry though he was, he hadn't planned on marching right onto the platform brandishing his wooden stick.

The *diak* was standing there in the doorway pondering his best course of action when one of the ushers approached and invited him to enter and have a seat. Not sure what else to do, the Orthodox *diak* left the stick outside, stepped in, and sat down.

On the platform, however, when the German pastor began preaching, he noticed that a Russian had come. He also recognized that this wasn't just any Russian, but a man who held a prominent position in the local Orthodox church.

Mary's parents Natalia (Mikhailovna Stragevitch) and Wladimir Ermacovitch in Brazil, 1929.

Even as the pastor preached, he quickly decided to make some changes in that morning's service. Instead of closing his meeting in the usual way, he asked the congregation to sing a hymn. While the people sang, he spoke to one of his members who understood Russian. He explained that there was a Russian in the service and that it was a man who didn't understand German. He asked his church member to give a short evangelistic message in Russian.

"Yes, I can do that," the church member agreed.

When the song ended, the pastor addressed his flock: "We have a Russian friend visiting today, and he does not speak German. So now we will have a short message in the Russian language."

While the German man opened God's Word in Russian, Natalia's father listened. Within a few minutes, this respected leader from the Orthodox church began hearing truths from the Scriptures that he had never encountered or considered before. As a result, instead of beating his daughter and dragging her back to the Orthodox church, he himself repented of sin and walked forward to receive Christ as Savior.

Later, when the Orthodox priest and his followers heard this news, they were both disappointed and furious. How dare the Baptists steal one of their leaders? But Natalia and her father rejoiced, and eventually all of the family became born-again Christians. In time her father started to preach among Slavic immigrants, and through his witness many people accepted Christ as Savior, were baptized, and organized Slavic Baptist churches. Because Mary's mother Natalia spoke fluently in Russian, German, and Portuguese, she would often interpret various preachers' sermons from one language to another. When her own daughter Maria (Mary) was sixteen, Maria heard about the new Russian language Bible Institute in Argentina from her uncle, Andres Prokopchuk who served as the academic dean. Though Mary's parents had reservations concerning their young daughter departing to study in another country at such a young age, eventually they agreed. In order to make this possible, Andres and Marta Prokopchuk became Mary's legal guardians, which allowed her to move to Argentina and enroll in the Russian Bible Institute.

So that's how it turned out that Mary was born and raised in a dedicated Christian home in Brazil, and which is also why Peter lovingly called her his *Brazilianka* ("Brazilian girl"). By the time she enrolled, Peter was finishing his studies, graduated, and then traveled far and wide to hold evangelistic meetings, not only in Argentina but also in Paraguay and Brazil. He became a well known and popular evangelist among the Slavic churches of South America.

Peter and Mary enjoyed telling two different versions of how they met at the Bible Institute in Argentina. Peter's version was that when Mary heard about him all the way from Brazil, she promptly left friends, family, and homeland to search for him in Argentina. Mary's version (far more convincing to family and friends alike) was that, considering Peter's shortage of musical abilities, his short-lived idea to return and take a class in music was a thinly veiled plan to seek out a wife from among the young female students.

Peter and Mary Slobodian. Many friends told Mary she resembled Evita Duarte Perón, wife of the Argentine president in the 1940s and 1950s.

Living in Sáenz Peña, the second largest city of Chaco province, Peter had also organized a Slavic Baptist church in that city before he got married. After their wedding, Mary joined him in ministering in that church, where he preached in Russian and Ukrainian. [5]

Slavic Baptist Church in Sáenz Peña.

5 Peter and a couple of helpers from the school had been working with this group of people for a while, so when he and Maria headed to Sáenz Peña, they were warmly welcomed by the church.

However, other churches around their city held services in other languages, such as Spanish, German, and Czech. These, too, invited Peter to participate in their ministries by holding evangelistic meetings and by supplying Bibles and other forms of literature in their languages. In this way, Peter and Mary's activities spread to other provinces of Argentina, and from there to Paraguay and Brazil. The two were frequently traveling from place to place and continued doing so even when they had children. He preached or gave his testimony to a wide variety of people, including some cults, Indians of the Toba and Matacos tribes, and Jewish people. The native peoples had never even seen a record player and were fascinated with it. Peter and Mary played musical records as part of their ministry, and this turned out to be an excellent tool for gathering native Indians together for Bible preaching and for teaching children's meetings. All he wanted was to reach these people for Jesus Christ, who had already reached *him.* [6]

Missionaries supported by and working with Slavic Gospel Association.

Throughout their ministry in South America they worked as missionaries in church-planting and evangelism under Slavic Gospel Association (SGA), which was founded by Peter Deyneka, who

[6] After their daughter Ann was born, Peter and Maria took her along on trips when possible, and people were amazed that they had trained her to stay on her little blanket. She watched as her father and mother took part in services and didn't stray from the blanket. There were no church nurseries in those days, and no disposable diapers, so traveling with children wasn't easy. When Ann and Sam were still young, they were left with their grandpa and grandma while Peter and Maria took longer or more "dangerous" types of journeys. One time, Peter and Maria were gone for three months, and Sam was so young that he wasn't sure who they were when they returned, which broke Maria's heart. After that, Peter and Maria tried to not schedule such long trips.

was a great inspiration for Peter. It was also SGA that sent the young Russian-speaking missionary Constantine Lewshenia from Chicago to preach in Argentina, resulting in the conversion of Peter and many others. This same Slavic Gospel Association established the Bible Institute in Argentina where Peter and Mary received their initial Bible training.

Building a house

At the start of their joint life together, Peter and Mary rented apartments for their homes. But moving from one apartment to another wasn't an easy chore. In time they concluded that they simply must acquire their own house, but that wasn't a simple accomplishment. To build any sort of house required money—a commodity the newlyweds didn't possess in great abundance. Ultimately they determined that, to reduce the cost of construction, they would perform as much of the manual labor as they could by themselves. For whatever tasks they couldn't perform personally, they would hire an experienced builder to do, but still using the materials they purchased cheaply.

The couple bought bricks directly from a factory, and they went to construction supply stores to locate less-expensive materials. At the point in construction when they were nearly ready for doors and windows, Peter traveled into a remote part of the forest, and there he preached among Indian tribes. In the same area, however, he also found immigrants from Spain. They were chopping down trees to fashion many objects out of wood. One of them was a

The house that Peter and Mary built in Sáenz Peña, Argentina.

carpenter who fashioned excellent doors and windows. So Peter asked that carpenter if he could make the doors and windows for Peter's house. The man set a price that was less expensive than Peter could have found elsewhere, so that is how he purchased windows and doors.

In addition, Peter and Mary had a helpful friend who was a contractor. That man arranged to acquire free permits and city rights without charging them. Plus, he directed them to a builder who helped to build their home much less expensively. In the end, they calculated that God had enabled them to get their own house for approximately half the normal price.

CHAPTER 6
Immigration to the United States

Over time Peter and Mary developed warm friendships with various American missionaries. Because Peter had a burning desire to deepen his knowledge of God's Word and to continue formal studies in it, he would sometimes bring up that topic with missionaries. They, in turn, told the couple about Bible colleges in the United States and about all the opportunities there to study the Scriptures in depth. Peter and Mary inquired about how they could go and study in such schools, but they soon discovered that studying in America would not be simple. Peter was told that he must write letters to Bible colleges in the United States and ask to be invited to come as a student. In order have any chance of enrolling in the U.S., the Americans advised Peter, "You must have English-speaking credentials."

The Slobodian Family, 1957.

However, despite his skill with other tongues, Peter didn't have any English-language credentials. Not to be stymied by that barrier, he signed up for a correspondence course and began studying English by mail. He did complete the course and received his diploma, a very large and beautiful diploma complete with ornate artwork, a photograph of Peter, and the words, "Diploma in Practical English." However, as one could imagine, he was destined for difficulties with a language he could read but not speak aloud. Nevertheless, once he had his English credentials in hand, Peter applied for admission to various schools. Imagine Peter and Mary's excitement when they received a letter from Northwestern College in Minnesota informing him that he had been accepted.

However, another complication was that, by this time, the couple had two children, Ann and Sam. Peter made several visits to the American Embassy in Buenos Aires in an attempt to navigate the bureaucracy of taking his family to the States. Representatives there explained that, because Peter was born in Ukraine, he would need to wait for a visa. The U.S. Department of Immigration set a maximum quota of Ukrainians accepted each year. They also warned that the waiting period could last several years. Rather than waiting so long to immigrate, Peter and Mary decided to go as students. In order to do that, they would need to leave their children with Peter's parents for the years that they would be studying. For Peter this wasn't unthinkable. After all, his own parents had left him in Ukraine. For Mary, however, peace about such a decision didn't come easily.

Peter returned to the American embassy and explained to an official that the two of them now planned to leave their children with his parents. Another man in the embassy was walking past and overheard part of this conversation. Curious, he joined the discussion.

"Why aren't you taking your children with you?" he wanted to know.

Peter explained to him about the quota problem.

The newcomer perused Peter's paperwork, then looked up with a smile. "I know a way that you can go as immigrants and still take your children with you. I see from your papers that you are a minister."

"Yes," Peter replied. "I spread the Gospel."

"You know what you can do? Find a church in the United States and ask them for help. The pastor of that church can send you an official invitation, and when you get those papers, you can get an immigrant visa, and your whole family will get to go together."

The Slobodian family packed all their belongings to head to America. In the rear right are grandma Hanka and grandpa Anton, saying farewell in Sáenz Peña.

Peter did exactly as that man instructed, and through his network of friends and contacts he located a willing Russian-speaking pastor in New York, Reverend Kisselov. That man mailed to them all that they required to get their immigrant visas.

Traveling to the U.S. in the most economical way possible, in 1957 Peter and his family flew on a Chilean two-motor airplane to Miami, Florida. From Miami they boarded another airplane bound for New York. Once there, Peter searched the crowd for whomever was supposed to pick them up. When he spotted a man holding a photograph of them, he knew it must be the pastor of the church.

Slobodian farewell sendoff from family and friends in Buenos Aires.

Peter and Mary thanked God, both for

that man in the American embassy who had given good advice and also for this helpful American pastor. The pastor hoped that they might remain in New York to work among Slavic immigrants in his church. However, they had come to pursue their education, and they stuck to that plan. Besides, Northwestern College in Minneapolis, Minnesota, had already accepted both of them as students. As soon as could be arranged, the Slobodian family purchased Greyhound bus tickets and began the long trek across America.

Experiences in Minneapolis

Peter and family arrived in Minneapolis, where they rented a small apartment about three blocks from the college. The apartment was on the fourth floor of an aging building. Of course, living on the fourth floor meant that they had to tramp up and down many steps, which was wearying. But the fourth-floor apartment was cheaper than those on the lower floors. With their limited finances, the family's higher quarters were the most practical.

The Slobodians arrive in the United States!

When the two parents searched for work, Mary had an advantage: in Argentina she had graduated from Teniente Academy, where she received her diploma in designing and sewing. In fact, had she remained in Argentina, she could have established her own school and taught girls the same profession. So when Mary went to look for work, she was hired that first day by the Jean Lang Dress Company. She was promoted quickly and became the seamstress who sewed each first sample dress as it came from the designer. She would suggest changes and would also suggest which fabric would work best for their designs. When she was pregnant with daughter Debbie, the dress company actually sent work home with Mary, which was unheard of in those days. Peter, however, didn't find a job so quickly. Whenever he applied for a job, the manager would ask what kind of work he had done before.

"I'm a preacher," he replied honestly.

"Barbers and preachers don't make good workers," was one manager's response.

Evidently other employers felt the same way. So Peter couldn't find a job. As a result, he entered the full program at Northwestern College while Mary worked full time that first year and took only a couple classes.

Before flying to the U.S., Peter had memorized quite a few useful English words from a dictionary. However, no American had helped him with pronunciation, and Peter didn't realize what tremendous differences exist between written words in Slavic languages and written words in English. In Russian and Ukrainian, every written letter plays a role in the pronunciation of a word. There are no silent *g*'s (as in the English word *gnat*), or silent *e*'s. And combining Cyrillic consonants does not give them a totally different sound (as happens with the English *enough* or *phone*.) As a result, when Peter tried to speak, Americans couldn't understand his so-called English. He, in turn, didn't understand their English replies.

For instance, when Peter wanted to say the word *knife*, he pronounced it letter by letter—including the *k* and the *e*. It took a while for him to unlearn all the incorrect pronunciations he had diligently committed to memory from a dictionary.

Before classes began, new students had to take entrance examinations. Peter was told he must take a test in spelling, mathematics, psychology, and other subjects. In later years Peter especially remembered the psychology test. It consisted of multiple-choice answers. For each question, there were five answers; four were wrong, and only one would be correct. The students also received special metal punch pins, with which they could punch holes to indicate their answers.

When the professor said, "Begin," the other students started punching their papers, so Peter started punching, too. At the end of the hour the professor said, "Stop."

Everybody halted, except for Peter. He continued punching. The professor was collecting everyone's papers, and when he reached Peter's seat, Peter was still punching. The professor stretched out his right hand, and Peter concluded that the man wanted to shake. So Peter obliged by shaking this man's hand but continued to punch holes. At last the professor said to him, "Please... Your paper." Peter stopped punching and surrendered his exam paper.

When Peter walked past that professor the next day, the man smiled at him. A few days later he invited Peter into his office.

"I know you're not experienced, and I understand you're from a different country. You don't know the language. I was a missionary in Africa, so I can understand how you feel."

It was nice to find someone who had already experienced the confusion and adjustments Peter was now going through.

Another time a different professor was lecturing in a Hermeneutics course. He gave the class a test. There were ten oral questions, and Peter missed two of them. Uncertain of the questions' meanings, he asked the professor to repeat them, but the professor would not oblige. Peter explained that if he didn't repeat them, he would flunk the test. Peter also explained that he had come from a distant country to study in the U.S. and to earn a degree.

The professor, however, would not budge. "Regardless of whether you pass the test or receive a degree, you'll still get an education." He didn't repeat the questions.

Later Peter complained about the incident to another professor. This other educator tried to console him, saying, "Don't worry, Peter. We don't understand him either."

However, Peter was extremely discouraged and on the verge of dropping out of school. He returned to their apartment, but Mary was out working. When she came home, she immediately sensed that something was wrong.

"What happened?" she asked.

He recounted how he had flunked the test. He also told her he had decided to drop out of school.

Mary would hear nothing of the kind. "We came to the United States to study, so tomorrow morning you are going back to school. You took a full load, so you must work hard."

When Peter heard his wife's tone, it reminded him of an incident that had happened to one of his friends. The friend had gotten into a disagreement with his wife, and the difference of opinion escalated into a heated argument. Just when the friend thought that he had the victory, it turned out otherwise. The wife grabbed a broom and was ready to swat him with it.

For protection, the man scrambled under the kitchen table.

The wife tried to push him out from under the table with her broom. "Come out of there!"

"I'm the head of this house," he shot back, "and if I want to come out, I will. But if I don't want to come out, then I'll stay under here."

Peter didn't want any victory such as that. So when Mary insisted, "You are going back to school," he answered, "Yes, ma'am!"

Mary added, "Next year I'm enrolling as well." The next morning he returned to classes. In later years he enjoyed retelling the story of Mary's "order" that he not drop out of school.

Of course, attending college without a solid grasp of the English language continued to be a struggle. To make the challenge even tougher, Peter's academic program required that he study yet other languages. Greek and Hebrew, which were extremely difficult, demanded much time and concentration. So, to bolster his understanding of English, Peter would memorize vocabulary words. To improve his spelling, he would hand-copy the New Testament. These disciplines enabled him to make good strides in his studies.

The following year, Mary became a full-time student too, and they began to accomplish their goals for coming to the United States. God was good and helped both of them to complete their class work, to pay for their tuition, and to pay the apartment rent. Both of them excelled in their studies and became top students. God also blessed them with a third child, Debbie, who was born on May 19, 1962—only two weeks before Mary graduated from Northwestern College with a B.A. in Missions. Peter enjoyed summarizing the family background as follows: "I was born in Ukraine, my wife Mary was born in Brazil, Ann and Sam were born in Argentina, and Debbie was born right here in Minneapolis. She is our 'real' American."

Mary earns her BA two weeks after Debbie was born. The Slobodians pose outside the apartment building on Spruce Street, where they lived on the fourth floor.

In the autumn of 1962 the Slobodians all did become U.S. citizens. That day, the whole family walked to the Minneapolis courthouse. For them, a long walk wasn't unusual since the Slobodians didn't own a car. The family's most common modes of transportation were walking or public transport. After they arrived at the courthouse, applications were filled out, and Peter and Mary took the required exam while Ann and Sam were "naturalized," which is the process that enables those of young age to become citizens along with their parents. Upon passing the exam, they all attended a swearing-in ceremony. That was a joyful day in the Slobodian household!

Starting a Slavic church

"Mary, look at this."

Peter had been flipping through the Minneapolis telephone directory and happened to notice a Slavic name. Looking closer, he had spotted another, then another. They recognized various Slavic nationalities by the family names.

There were Polish names such as Cominski, Ghensicki, and Mosticki.

They found Ukrainian names such as Shevchenko, Tovstenko, and Pohodenko.

Russian names included Prochanov, Kisilov, and Kozlov.

They found Byelorussian names, too, such as Tatarchuk, Procopchuk, and Shevchuk.

Peter and Mary were astounded. "There must be thousands of Slavic immigrants in this city!" But out of those thousands, how many of them had repented of their sin and placed their faith in Jesus Christ for salvation? How many had even heard about God's plan of salvation?

Perhaps American preachers couldn't speak all those languages from Eastern Europe, but Peter and Mary could. They decided to locate some of these people to meet them. So they did. With no advance notice, they dropped by these immigrants' homes, introduced

Slavic Baptist Church group photo.

themselves, and established friendships. Then they offered to start a Bible study with their new friends. They even began preaching services right in people's homes. When people got saved, Peter would baptize them, and eventually he organized Slavic Baptist Church with these new believers as members.

The congregation named their church Slavic Baptist because it consisted of people from multiple Slavic nationalities, not just one. Peter regularly preached in three or four different languages in order to nourish this interesting flock with spiritual food. At first the fledgling group had no building of their own, so they rented denominational church buildings for their services.

Then Peter and Mary discovered a neighborhood where numerous Ukrainian people lived, so he and Mary organized Ukrainian Baptist Church there. While Mary was earning money for their needs, these new churches started to support Peter's ministry financially. It was a blessed work. Talented musicians joined the churches, and wonderful choirs developed. They also had many active young people. Those churches are doing God's work to this day.

When Peter and Mary moved away from Minneapolis, the Slavic Baptist Church became predominantly Polish, because members from other Slavic nationalities moved away too. This church called a pastor from Poland, and he served there a few years before he went home to be with the Lord. Then they called another pastor from Poland. The Ukrainian Baptist Church also needed a pastor, and they invited one from Brazil.

Later, when the Soviet Union collapsed, these churches expanded rapidly, because many Baptist Christians from that land immigrated to the West in the 1990s and joined them.

One of the professors at Northwestern was Dr. R.V. Clearwaters, pastor of the large and influential Fourth Baptist Church of Minneapolis. The very next year after Peter graduated, Dr. Clearwaters established Central Baptist Theological seminary. Peter enrolled in Central Baptist Seminary for its very first year and eventually received two more degrees, an M.Div and his Th.M. During those years, Peter and Mary developed many life-long friendships with students who went on to serve as pastors, missionaries, and evangelists.

One of the more memorable events from this period was Peter's ordination. Though Peter had been ordained a Baptist minister in Argentina, one of the professors suggested to him that it wouldn't be a bad idea to be ordained in the United States. After all, that would not be a problem, especially since Peter was already in the ministry and pastoring the immigrant churches he had started in Minneapolis.

Peter receiving his diploma from Dr. Richard V. Clearwaters.

Realizing that the procedure for an ordination could be different in the United States, Peter asked the professor how to proceed. He was told that his church would need to take action and vote to hold an ordination council, in which ordained ministers from other churches would interview Peter on points of doctrine. Once they were satisfied that

Peter's graduating class from Central Baptist Seminary.

he was of sound doctrine and had a solid grasp of theology, they would make a recommendation to the church for his official ordination. When Peter asked which pastors should be invited besides those connected with the seminary and Fourth Baptist Church, the answer was a vague "pastors from the area." Of course, the professor meant Baptist pastors of like faith and practice. However, Peter interpreted this to mean he should look in the telephone book and select a few pastors of churches that were near the Slavic church he had established. When some who were selected randomly from the phone book appeared at the ordination on January 28, 1964, the differing views they held on various doctrinal points provided for some lively discussion among the pastors who assembled to interview Peter. Nevertheless, there were plenty of established and well-known ordained Baptist ministers present in the council who, upon thoroughly examining Peter's doctrine and Bible knowledge, enthusiastically recommended that the church ordain Peter.

Peter was ordained in Minneapolis, Minnesota, on January 28, 1964.

Following are the signatures that appear on the ordination document: Charles G. Pausley (Council Moderator), F. Donald Worden (Council Clerk), Alexander Mezak (Church Clerk), Ernest Pickering, H.S. Murphy, R.W. Myrant, Richard V. Clearwaters, M. James Hollowood, John G. Stock, Frank M. Peterson, Palmer A. Yngsdad, Roger Terry, Robert C. Opfer, Warren Vanhetloo, H.E. Thorn, Roger L. Peterson, and Robert G. Delnay. Peter was pleased to associate with such fundamentalist preachers, who shared the same separatist position from worldliness and liberalism that Peter had learned in the Scriptures.

Those years in Minneapolis, which combined Bible college and seminary studies with planting Slavic churches, were busy and fruitful years.

Moving to Chicago

When Peter and Mary finished their schooling in Minnesota, they pondered where to go next. Their desire was to minister in the Soviet Union, but at the time that door was closed. Ukraine was under the control of Communism, and the communists certainly would not allow missionaries to come and preach the Gospel.

Because the Slobodians couldn't move to the USSR, the couple's next desire was to return to South America. But about that time the *Minneapolis Tribune* printed an article about immigrants who relocated to the United States. Thanks to that feature article, Peter understood that there were not thousands, but *millions*, of immigrants settling in the United States.

"The United States is a great and needy mission field," Peter would say. "Not only among English-speaking citizens, but also among immigrants." Still desiring to reach people from Eastern Europe with the Gospel, Peter and Mary applied to serve as missionaries under a Baptist mission board. They were accepted; however, for whatever reason, invitations to preach and candidate in churches simply didn't develop easily at all. Just when Peter was wondering if he should be doing something differently, Baptist World Missions approached him and invited him to minister with BWM, which had been organized just a few years before, in 1961. In addition, BWM offered to help Peter schedule meetings in churches. After a time of both discussion and prayer, Peter and Mary accepted this invitation.

Anton and Hanka Slobodian eventually joined Peter and family in Chicago, where Anton lived out the rest of his days.

The Slobodians' target group would be immigrants to the U.S. When Peter studied various cities with large immigrant populations, he learned what wide-open possibilities for ministry existed in Chicago. Among the immigrants in that metropolis were multitudes of Russians, Byelorussians, Czechs, Ukrainians, Poles, and other Slavic people.

Peter was astounded to learn that, in all the world, Chicago is the city with the second-largest population of Poles. Only Warsaw, Poland, has more Polish people than Chicago. So this Midwestern city seemed like the ideal base for missionaries with multiple languages at their disposal. In 1966, the family moved from Minneapolis to Chicago and immediately began searching for Slavic immigrants.

As he had done in Minneapolis, Peter opened a telephone book and scanned its pages for familiar-sounding names. Just like before, he and Mary drove to peoples' houses, introduced themselves, shared their faith, started Bible studies, and eventually began preaching in homes.

As people came to Christ for salvation, he baptized them and organized churches. Typically the new churches would start by renting an existing church building during hours when the home congregation wasn't using it.

One Sunday, when Peter was preaching in the Ukrainian Baptist Church of Chicago, two Hispanic-looking men entered the auditorium and took seats in a pew. As soon as he saw them, Peter realized from their faces that they were Hispanic.

"Perhaps they understand some Ukrainian," Peter thought. He knew of cases where Hispanic people who worked alongside Ukrainians had learned some of the language.

After the service, Peter approached the strangers and greeted them in Ukrainian.

One of them replied, *"No comprendo,"* which means, "I don't understand."

So Peter greeted them in Spanish instead. The men were startled when Peter effortlessly shifted from Ukrainian to their Spanish, which are quite different languages from each other.

"We're Catholics," they told him. "But we wanted to find out how Baptists conduct their services."

Peter jotted down the address of a Spanish-language Baptist church in Chicago and suggested that they would get more benefit from visiting those services.

Before they left, however, one of these two men offered a final comment. "You speak our language. Why don't you work among Spanish-speaking people?"

In the days that followed, that question kept echoing in Peter's heart: "Why don't you work among Spanish-speaking people?" It was an excellent question. Although Spanish wasn't Peter's first tongue, his years in Argentina had made him more than fluent enough to teach and preach in Spanish. Besides, this was now the 1970s, and the old Ukrainian neighborhoods of Chicago were beginning to change. While ministering among Chicago's Slavic population, he noticed that there was no longer a continual trickle of immigrants coming from Communist countries. Due to the Cold War, the flow of immigrants from Eastern Europe had dried up. Furthermore, the children of earlier immigrants grew up speaking English, so they really didn't need to hear sermons in the "old country" languages of their parents and grandparents.

Even though the flow of Slavic immigrants coming to Chicago drastically dropped at the onset of the Cold War, this didn't immediately affect the ethnic neighborhoods of the city. However, by the late 1970s the aging Slavic population began to diminish rapidly. Formerly Slavic neigh-

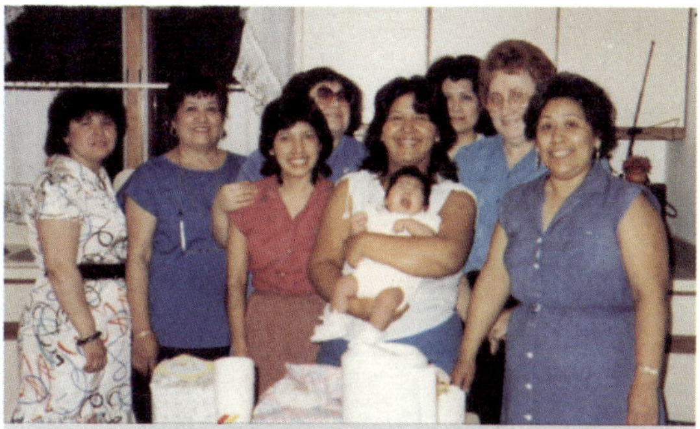

Having lived in Latin America, Mary had the Spanish language skills necessary to fit naturally into the Hispanic ministry in Chicago. Here she's fellowshipping with several ladies in one of their homes.

borhoods began to take on an increasingly Hispanic identity. So, as some immigrants died and others moved away, Peter had already noticed his mission field among Slavic people was dissipating before his eyes. He was right at this stage of ministry when the Hispanic visitor asked why he didn't labor among people who speak Spanish.

"It's the Macedonian Call," he told Mary.

"All right then, let's work with Spanish-speaking people," she agreed.

That decision settled a matter that had been growing on Peter's heart.

So Peter and Mary now turned their attention to a huge and thriving mission field that was all around them: the Hispanic residents of Chicago. They began this Hispanic phase of ministry the same way they had begun earlier Slavic outreaches—by personally calling on people in their apartments and their houses.

"We began to work on the north side of Chicago, starting a Bible study and later preaching services. People repented and got saved," Peter later summarized. In actual fact, Peter found it easier to win converts among the Hispanics. Russians and Ukrainians came for-

First Fundamental Baptist Church.

ward only rarely to accept Christ as Savior in services. Hispanics, on the other hand, didn't hesitate. Once the Holy Spirit gripped their hearts, they would immediately walk down the aisles to express their desire to repent and accept Christ as Lord.

Peter baptized the new converts and organized a local church, *Primera Iglesia Bautista Fundamental* (First Fundamental Baptist Church). The next step was to teach the new believers how to reach their own people with the Gospel. Peter would accompany men, and Mary would lead women as they hit the streets to win souls. Anytime someone accepted Christ, Peter and Mary would ask that new believer to take them to homes of unsaved friends or relatives where the new believers could share God's Word and how it had changed their lives.

Food and fellowship with Spanish-speaking believers.

However, the Slobodians quickly learned that the apartments of Hispanics could be quite different from those of people from Eastern Europe. The decorations were different, of course, but their cooking was spicy, much more peppery than dishes from Eastern Europe or Argentina.

"The air in their apartments was so hot and spicy that when I was in some of them I felt like I might pass out," Peter recalled. However, being polite and not wanting to offend the host and hostess, he kept silent about his own discomfort. "But their own people had more courage and asked them to open a door to get some air flowing." Emboldened by the example of his new Hispanic friends, Peter learned to ask people to open their doors—not just to let him in, but sometimes so that he could stand to stay inside once invited!

First Fundamental Baptist Church grew, and its members conducted an active young people's ministry. They also invited Bible students from Maranatha Baptist Bible College in Watertown, Wisconsin, to come and help in various ways.

Peter with baptismal candidates.

"We began a bus ministry," Peter later recalled, "bringing to church people who didn't have their own transportation. People learned to serve the Lord financially through tithing, giving offerings, and Faith Promise giving."

But even at this point the church was still renting facilities for their services and activities. Eventually the members brought up the subject of buying their own building. Peter was heartened to hear that they wanted to take this next step in the life of their church. But he had a question for them.

The new building purchased on North Damen Avenue, Chicago.

"Where will the money for our building come from?"

The initial response that several people offered wasn't the best one: "You should get money from American churches," they told Peter.

He shook his head. "It's your own responsibility to provide for your own building."

So the church accepted that responsibility and began setting aside money toward their goal. When the Ukrainian Baptist Church in Berwyn decided to move elsewhere and to put their building up for sale, the Spanish-speaking congregation was immediately interested. They made an acceptable offer and purchased that church on North Damen Avenue in Chicago.

Next Peter and Mary turned their sights on Spanish speakers on the south side of Chicago. In addition, they even traveled to Rockford, Illinois, and assisted with a Spanish outreach there. Because he couldn't effectively pastor First Fundamental Baptist Church while planting new churches elsewhere, Peter invited his brother Nicolas in Argentina to come and take over leadership of that congregation.

Describing his ministry among speakers of Spanish, Peter once declared, "Working with Spanish people is a blessing. They want you

Peter preaching mini-sermons between songs in Humboldt Park, Chicago.

to teach them, and they put it into practice. They are wonderful people. The city of Chicago is truly a great mission field. It is well known for its ethnic make-up. Many sections of the city can be identified by their own distinctive nationalities. The Hispanic population is the fastest growing minority group with over one million Spanish-speaking people. Thank the Lord for those with a burden for the city of Chicago!"

For residents of the Humboldt Park section of the city, Peter must have been an intriguing man to observe in action. On Sunday afternoons Peter and his family and other believers drove to this particular park to evangelize, because the surrounding neighborhood was home to various nationalities. While fellow Christians performed attention-getting musical numbers and a crowd gathered around, Peter would mingle with the bystanders to hear what language most people were speaking. If he heard a lot of Ukrainian, after a few musical numbers, he would step forward, open his Bible, and preach in Ukrainian. At the end of that sermon, the musicians would play other hymns and songs. Some people walked away, but others would join the group of bystanders and listen. Again Peter would mingle and find out which language was being spoken most. So next he might switch and preach in Russian. After that, depending on the predominant tongue in the crowd around him, he might open a Polish Bible or a Spanish Bible and continue preaching in those languages!

Musicians playing between sermons
in Humboldt Park, Chicago.

By the time the Slobodian family piled into the car for the drive home, Peter's brain would be exhausted. Preaching in so many diverse languages was taxing. But just when he wanted to rest his mind, Mary would want to discuss foreign grammar. Because she, too, understood several languages, she sometimes wanted to correct a grammatical construction that Peter had used in Polish, or Ukrainian, or Spanish.

"Not right now," Peter would reply softly. "After preaching so long, my mind is worn out. Tell me about it tomorrow."

Of course, by the next day, Mary would have forgotten which point of grammar she had intended to critique. And that, Peter eventually confessed, was exactly what he was counting on.

Around that time, the California Graduate School of Theology was one of the first schools to introduce advanced degrees in theology offered in "modular" sessions, which meant that students could enroll without leaving their full-time ministries since these classes were in held in shorter modular segments. Peter and Mary arranged to stay with Peter's sister Olga and mother (who had also immigrated by that time and lived together) in the Los Angeles area during the weeks that the couple attended classes. In this way, Peter and Mary received Ph.D.'s in 1973, and Peter received his Th.D. in 1975. At the same time, their periodic absences provided aspiring preachers back in Chicago with opportunities to take turns in the pulpit.

Peter graduates from California Graduate School of Theology with a Th.D. in 1975.

Globe-trotting

Because Peter and Mary had lived so many years in South America, after living in the United States for a number of years, they wanted to go back and visit that continent. In addition, they wanted to visit Mary's mother, who was dying of leukemia at the time. So, in 1972, they flew south again. As it turned out, Mary's mother passed away before they arrived, which they regretted, but the trip was to provide many other blessings for them. Peter particularly wished to hold evangelistic services. He arranged meetings via his Russian Bible Institute contacts. First the couple headed to Argentina. In Buenos Aires, the capital of Argentina, Peter preached many times and saw souls saved. From there they proceeded on to other provinces, where he preached in various languages. From Paraguay, they traveled to Brazil, then on to Uruguay as well, meeting and spending time with some American missionaries. In each place Peter preached salvation from sin through Jesus Christ. "We had a blessed time," Peter reported. Then they returned to the United States, where they resumed work among Slavic and Spanish-speaking people.

Peter and Mary visiting his home church, where he was saved.

A few years later they returned to South America, and Peter preached in a similar series of services in Argentina, Paraguay, Uruguay, and Brazil. Because Peter had been a popular evangelist before he left for the U.S., people far and wide had warm memories of the Slobodians. Thus, their missionary work wasn't in just one country, but in several countries and in several languages to various ethnic people groups, including Indians of the Tobas and Matatcos tribes. (Peter formally studied and learned eight languages in classrooms, but had picked up some others by studying on his own.)

On this second trip to South America they enjoyed the same opportunities as on the first return visit: Peter held evangelistic meetings and preached in numerous churches. He preached or gave his testimony to a wide variety of people. All he wanted was to reach these people for Jesus Christ, who had already reached *him*.

CHAPTER 7
Reaching out to Russia

In the later 1970s, while Peter was serving in Chicago as a church planter among Slavic and Spanish-speaking people under Baptist World Mission, the seed of an idea took root in his thoughts and began to grow. Thrilled though he was to see people in the Chicago area come to Christ, an unfulfilled aspiration still lay heavily on his heart: He longed to fulfill the Great Commission among the Slavic people of the Soviet Union. But how was that possible?

Peter prayed and thought much about it. Then he contemplated the fact that one pipeline for communicating the Gospel to communistic countries was wide open—radio ministry. He learned that in the Soviet Union almost every household owned a shortwave radio. Why? Because citizens of the USSR didn't trust their own news media. They wanted to hear what

People gathered around a shortwave radio in the USSR.

was happening in other parts of the world, outside the Iron Curtain. The only direct access to foreign news was via shortwave radio broadcasts, which traveled many times the distance of regular AM or FM radio signals.

If the Soviet government wouldn't permit a missionary to relocate to the Soviet Union to evangelize, then why not evangelize the Union of Soviet Socialist Republics from America? Peter could tape-record Russian and Ukrainian sermons, and then broadcast them to the USSR via shortwave radio. In fact, upon further consideration, Peter realized that shortwave radio messages could potentially reach an audience far more vast than one missionary could ordinarily hope to touch in a lifetime.

"What a great opportunity to preach, reaching people who cannot be reached in any other way!"

He committed this dream to the Lord in prayer. Weighing the pros and cons of radio evangelism, Peter turned to various friends and colleagues for advice. However, Peter's vision for evangelizing the Soviet bloc by radio encountered resistance among colleagues at Baptist World Mission. Of course, these friends were certainly not opposed to Russians and Eastern Europeans hearing the Gospel. However, that decade was the seventies. During that era, a number of formerly fundamental ministries were departing from church-planting in favor of liberal or social-Gospel approaches to ministry. In order to avoid such tangents by its workers, BWM had drafted a policy that its missionaries would engage only in hands-on, local church-planting. Because a radio ministry didn't fit that descrip-

Young man listening to *The Scripture Saith* on the radio.

tion, they politely requested that Peter refrain from radio ministry and to spend his time only in local evangelism and church-planting.

Peter listened to these colleagues' positions and understood the reasoning behind them, but he also listened to godly men who caught a vision for the enormous potential of winning souls for Jesus via the airwaves. In his heart, Peter felt that the Lord was urging him personally to push forward with this idea, to use his extraordinary repertoire of languages to preach to the widest possible number of listeners. At the same time, though, he didn't wish to cause division or strife within his own mission agency. What to do?

In April 1979 a notable leader of underground Baptist churches in the USSR, Georgi Vins, was released from a Siberian prison and exiled to the United States. Peter traveled to visit Georgi Vins and asked for his opinion concerning preaching by shortwave. Georgi Vins, who had grown up in the Soviet Union and suffered much persecution for his faith, affirmed that radio did indeed offer preachers a powerful tool for evangelizing. He advised that, if Peter had enough support to enter into such a ministry, then he should certainly do it.

In fact, as he traveled and preached, Georgi Vins occasionally shared a story from his own labor-camp experiences that involved radio ministry. One winter night in a labor camp, during a period in which Brother Vins felt particularly exhausted and discouraged, the Lord used a radio to encourage him in a nearly miraculous way. In the middle of the night, a guard appeared besides Vins's bunk and told him he was summoned to the camp office. Although weary and desperately in need of sleep, he rose and plodded across the compound to the office. There, the officer on night duty had been listening to the shortwave radio when he stumbled across a Russian church service being broadcast from South Korea. On impulse, he had sent a guard to summon his Christian prisoner.

"Would you like to listen awhile?"

"Yes, please," replied an incredulous Vins.

In this way, in the middle of the night, in the least likely of all places, Georgi Vins was able to receive spiritual nourishment and strengthening by means of radio preaching. When the ministers on the radio prayed, he bowed and prayed with them. When they sang Christian hymns in Russian, he quietly joined in singing praises to God. From time to time the duty officer checked on him, but other than that, no one disturbed Vins. When the program ended, he returned to his bunk with rejoicing in his heart. Such an experience had never occurred to him before, and it never occurred again in all his eight years of prisons and labor camps. Just when this servant of the Lord most needed uplifting, God used an atheistic officer and a shortwave radio to do it. So it is no wonder that Georgi Vins was in favor when Peter Slobodian asked for his thoughts concerning Christian radio work.

A few pastors said to Peter, "What are you waiting for? Start your own mission. God will help you."

"Form a new mission?" Peter pondered that suggestion. Such a proposal had never been part of his plans. He carried the matter to the Lord in prayer. Should he, or shouldn't he? As the Lord continued to lead Peter's thoughts, a plan of action began to develop. Now instead of simply pondering whether a radio work was feasible, his prayers became much more pointed: "God, help me to have a radio ministry."

5718 North Maplewood, Chicago, the home where BIEM was started and many of the first meetings were conducted.

And the Lord answered. Peter asked a number of pastors and businessmen to consider prayerfully whether they could serve on the Board of Directors of an entirely new mission. Some declined, but others accepted. In 1981 Peter invited the men who were willing to serve as board members of the new ministry to his home in Chicago. At that meeting they organized a mission agency, which they named Baptist International Evangelistic Ministries. Peter was designated as General Director. Others to accept positions on the original board were Dr. Ben Strohbehn, Dr. W.R. Martin, Dr. Harold Reemstma, Dr. L.D. Earnhart, Mr. Elbert Dean, Pastor Charles Surrett, and Pastor Sam Slobodian, Peter's son who was pastoring a church in Chicago.

That day was one of wonderful rejoicing in Peter's life. "Now God will help me to reach millions of people by radio and to get into their homes with the proclamation of the Word of God!"

Peter immediately began to plan a trip to the Soviet Union. He wanted to see up close the audience that such radio broadcasts would be targeting. By going to Russia, he would be able to rub shoulders with ordinary people and with pastors and thus gain insight into how to shape his sermons as well as an evaluation of how best to structure the programs as a whole. So in 1982 he, Mary, and their son Sam made their first flight to the Soviet Union. They traveled as tourists, but once there they began to seek out Christians. In conversations with both pastors and laymen, Peter posed the identical questions. What did they think of the effectiveness of Gospel radio broadcasts in their own language on international shortwave radio? Do people listen? Are such broadcasts interesting to hear? Do they attract many listeners? There were other questions as well, particularly for pastors: What should the programs emphasize, preaching or music—and in what proportion?

The response was unanimous and extremely encouraging. People told him, "When you go back to the United States, we want to hear your voice on the radio." Peter also met and fellowshipped with several individuals who were saved through radio preaching and had become members of local churches. Seeing such "living fruit" of another radio ministry burdened his heart all the more to preach by shortwave. So

Peter gained peace and confidence that radio ministry truly was effective and that the Lord was preparing him for a new phase in his life.

With God's help and with funding supplied by concerned believers in America, the new-born BIEM purchased all the necessary equipment to record and edit radio sermons. Of course, BIEM didn't own its own shortwave transmitter. But God's people provided sufficient funds to purchase airtime on existing radio stations, so that is how Peter's messages were broadcast.

In a preliminary radio announcement, Peter told listeners about an upcoming program that would be called "The Scripture Saith." Then he provided the times and frequencies for the broadcast and added that the programs are supported by Baptist believers in the United States through Baptist International Evangelistic Ministries.

Peter in the recording studio, taping a sermon. He hadn't been in the Soviet Union for decades, but by means of shortwave radio, his sermons could cross borders that he himself couldn't.

Peter's radio programs were completely different from other programs. The existing Russian Christian programs that were then on the air included much singing, reciting of Christian poems, and short sermons. However, when he was in the Soviet Union, Peter asked pastors what kind of broadcasts they would prefer to hear. They replied, "Dr. Pyotr Antonovich,[7] give us expository preaching. People do not own Bibles. They need to hear the Word of God." In response to that plea, BIEM's

7 In Russian, the English name "Peter" is pronounced "Pyotr," and a person's middle name is always derived from his or her father's name, never a random decision by the parents. Thus, "Pyotr Antonovich" basically equals Peter, son of Anton, and was a courteous way for any Russian speaker who wasn't closely acquainted to address Peter Antonovich Slobodian.

radio programs began with only a brief introduction, followed by twenty-eight minutes of preaching.

Peter and Sam began to make father and son trips to the Soviet Union. This resulted in establishing friendships and relationships with pastors and churches behind the Iron Curtain. On those trips they would meet with believers, preach in churches, and bring in Bibles and other Christian literature, plus aid for families of imprisoned Christians prisoners. On one trip, they connected with a couple from England who were doing the same. Christians in the USSR were delighted to welcome such visitors from the West. The Slobodians were blessed to become acquainted with this couple.

Peter and Sam Slobodian in Moscow, Russia.

However, there was serious advice to be heeded concerning such trips. For instance, what to say and what not to say to authorities, customs agents, and Intourist travel agency personnel. Intourist was only the travel agency in the Soviet Union in those days, and one had to be quite cautious in dealing with them since it was common knowledge that they were controlled by the KGB, which was interested in exploiting tourists for propaganda purposes.

Various Christians who already had experience with traveling to the USSR warned visiting Americans never to accept correspondence to carry over the border, not even from fellow believers. In those days it wasn't uncommon for tourists visiting from the West to be asked to mail a letter once they returned home. Many people in the Soviet Union wanted to communicate with relatives or acquaintances in the West. However, because of heavy mail censorship by the communist authorities, such letters almost never made it past the border. In fact, even attempting to mail a letter to the West could immediately put the sender under suspicion. Therefore, visitors from the West like the Slobodians and this couple from England were warned not to accept such letters, even from Christians. In fact, they were told that if they were caught with such a letter, as unpleasant as it would be for them as they faced possible arrest or deportation by the KGB, the penalty would be far worse for the letter's sender, who could be charged with criminal activity by the communist authorities. Such an attempt to communicate with the West could be interpreted as an act of treason.

Before long, the Slobodians were to learn just how real the danger was. On one of this British couple's visits to a Russian Christian home, they were asked to mail a letter. They immediately declined saying, "We can't take this letter with us. If we are caught with it, not only will we have problems, but it will be far worse for you." The family responded by saying, "We are not asking you to try to smuggle this out of the Soviet Union. Simply mail it from an ordinary mailbox here in Russia when you are not being watched. Sometimes letters do get past the censors. But since father is in prison, we are under surveillance. We can't mail this letter without being noticed. If someone else mailed the letter, at least there would be a slight chance it would get to the West."

Concluding that this would not be a problem, the couple accepted the letter and waited for a moment when they saw an inconspicuous mailbox. After a quick glance around, they dropped it into the slot and then continued walking. That evening there was a knock at their hotel room door. It was the KGB—with that very letter!

"Did you mail this?" the officer asked with a rock-hard, no-nonsense expression.

With sinking hearts, the couple looked at each other, then answered with the truth. "Yes."

At that reply, the KGB officer said, "You are under arrest for helping to disseminate anti-Soviet slander. Pack your things. You are going to be deported immediately."

When the Slobodians heard that story, they gained a new appreciation for all the precautionary steps they always took while inside the USSR. For instance, whenever they met with Christians in hotel rooms, or even in homes, whenever the topic concerned sensitive matters, the communication shifted to hand-written notes, since they understood that the conversations were likely monitored. But even in casual conversation with believers outdoors, one had to be careful. In those days, according to some sources, the Soviet secret police gleaned information from as many as thirty million people who underwent questioning concerning the activities of their neighbors, colleagues at work, and even other family members.

While the arrest of this couple didn't affect the Slobodians on that trip, the next time they applied for tourist visas they were rejected without explanation. Evidently the Slobodians' Christian activities had been monitored, perhaps even connected to their association with the arrested British couple. Furthermore, by then Peter was on the air, preaching the Gospel by radio. Very possibly the atheistic authorities didn't appreciate those radio broadcasts. Regardless of the cause, though, the door for visiting had slammed shut for these radio evangelists.

Missionary tour to England, Germany, Yugoslavia, Austria, Hungary, Czechoslovakia, and Poland

When Peter and Sam's plans for traveling back to the Soviet Union fell through, they wasted no time before considering other options for a missionary trip. After all, the USSR wasn't the only nation in Eastern Europe that needed to hear the Gospel. Even if they couldn't personally take Bibles into the Soviet Union itself, there was still a great need to get Bibles to nearby Soviet bloc countries. Furthermore,

Interesting Moments From Slobodian Family History

Peter with Sam, standing at the border of Hlibiv.

Greek Orthodox church in Hlibiv that the Slobodians attended.

House in Hlibiv similiar to the Slobodian home.

School in Hlibiv that Peter attended as a boy.

Peter fetching water on the homestead in Argentina.

Peter and Nicholas with parents in Chaco, Argentina.

Peter with plow behind an 8-horse team.

The Lewshenia family in Argentina.

Russian Bible Institute in Funes, Argentina. Mary is in the second row.

Peter's early ministry photo.

Farewell photo with family in Chaco, Argentina, 1957.

Slobodians boarding the airplane for the U.S. in 1957.

Slobodian family at Peter's graduation from Central Baptist Seminary in Minneapolis, Minn.

Slobodian Family Picture September 1963.

Slobodian family photo around 1969.

Peter and Mary's 25th anniversary.

Poster advertising Peter's evangelistic meetings in Russia.

Peter and Mary's prayer card.

Mary packing Bibles to send to Radio listeners in the Soviet Union.

BIEM headquarters building in Oak Forest, Illinois.

Peter and Mary's last portrait together.

BIEM's current home, Danville, Indiana.

Slobodian family portrait in 2001.

in some of those Eastern European nations there were contacts willing to transport Russian-language Bibles the rest of the way into the USSR. In this the Slobodians saw an opportunity to continue getting Bibles behind what was then called "the Iron Curtain." So the pair examined a map of Europe and began laying plans for an itinerary that would take them through nearby countries instead.

Their first stop on that trip was London, England. There, father and son visited that same British man and wife who, like BIEM,

Peter and Sam Slobodian in London.

were working to save souls and help Christians in Eastern Europe and the USSR.

After visiting London, Peter and Sam flew on to Germany. There they met with personal friends who were American missionaries. While in Germany, Peter and Sam preached in several churches, including Russian-speaking congregations of immigrants who had left the Soviet Union.

From Germany they traveled to Yugoslavia, as they had planned, then farther to Austria, where they were given an address of a contact living in Hungary who was a prospect for getting Bibles into Russia due to his work, which often brought him to Russian cities. The Slobodians' task was to meet with this contact whom they couldn't telephone in advance. (They later learned that he had applied for a telephone twenty-five years earlier and was still waiting!) The city they needed to go to was Miskolc, near the border. However, to get to anywhere in Hungary, one almost always had to go through Budapest. So the Slobodians, bearing large suitcases that contained a supply of Bibles for Russia, arrived by train in this large capital city.

When they arrived at the train station, they learned with dismay that they couldn't communicate with Hungarians at all. Earlier, Peter had no problem communicating in all the other countries they had visited because he either knew the language or because other Slavic languages were similar enough to ones he spoke that he could communicate on a basic level. However, Hungarian wasn't a Slavic language. It wasn't even closely related, and therefore efforts to communicate with Hungarians failed completely.

Knowing that they had to get to another train station to board the train from Budapest to Miskolc, Sam found a cab driver and drew a picture of a train and railroad tracks and repeated "Miskolc." The cab driver nodded his head emphatically and motioned for the two men to climb in. When he dropped them off, however, they learned too late that they were at the wrong train station! This time, though, there were some friendly Polish people at the station who were happy to assist the Slobodians in getting to the correct train for Miskolc.

Upon arriving at the railroad station in Miskolc, as soon as the Slobodians exited the train they noticed a profound difference in their surroundings. Budapest was a huge, cosmopolitan city bustling with foreigners from all over the world, so the Slobodian men didn't feel much out of place. However, it was clear from the moment the Slobodians stepped off the train in Miskolc that they were no longer in a large, cosmopolitan center. In addition, the stares they drew provided evidence that they were far from inconspicuous. This small city wasn't accustomed to foreign visitors, and they could see even that simply standing there with large suitcases (which were packed with Russian Bibles) was attracting quite a bit of unwanted attention. Making matters far worse, this time there were no friendly Polish people around to help.

Regardless of which language Peter or Sam used, each time people would shake their heads and reply, "Magyar," which meant they spoke only Hungarian. Even though the Slobodians had begun to solicit prayers for this journey months before, it was difficult to stay relaxed when every effort to find anyone they could communicate with in the train station proved futile.

As time passed, the situation grew worse when the lights in the station began to dim. Obviously, they would have to leave the station soon, and the two Slobodian men could already imagine themselves ending up in the police station and having to explain what they were doing in this town. In those times, foreign visitors were required to register at the local police within forty-eight hours of their arrival. Foreigners engaging in missions like the Slobodians were careful to make their necessary contacts and to leave town before the forty-eight hours expired. Therefore, the first logical step any local citizen might take in assisting the Slobodians would be to lead them straight to the police station to register. They weren't eager for a conversation with police, who might inquire why they needed such enormous suitcases if they planned to be there such a short time. Especially since the authorities had every right to inspect all luggage and often relished an opportunity to hunt for contraband. When illegal items were found, the police could either demand bribes or else score points with superiors by apprehending the offenders.

As the Slobodians stood there discussing what to say to the authorities, a large man approached them and very slowly said, "You speak English? I speak English." Peter and Sam rejoiced to hear these words. They felt nearly ready to hug this man who turned out to be very kind.

The stranger continued to speak slowly and deliberately. Since Peter and Sam were limited in what information they could share about their purpose, they simply said that they needed help in finding an address of someone they wanted to visit. The man pondered the situation and then spoke again, still slowly and carefully. "I will help you...will take all evening... Will call wife." In that part of the world it wasn't at all unusual to need an entire evening to locate one address. With so many unmarked streets, even a professional taxi cab driver could spend hours trying to find an address.

When asked how he learned English, the man explained that several months earlier, for some unknown reason he felt an urge to study English. His family, friends, and colleagues couldn't understand why he would want to pursue such a task. Furthermore, there in Miskolc he couldn't find any classes or instructor for the English language. However, he couldn't rest until he found an English-language instruction book and began to teach himself. Sam and Peter were moved as they came to realize, that months before they arrived, right at the same time they were requesting prayer for this journey, God was preparing the way before them by prompting this man to learn English. In fact, they later learned that when that man uttered to Peter and Sam the words, "You speak English… I speak English," that was the *first time* he had actually used the English he had been teaching himself!

At this point their Hungarian companion telephoned his wife and explained that he would be late, because he had decided not only to help them locate the address but also to check them into a hotel. The man handed Peter his business card, and Peter saw that he was highly educated and had a Ph.D. The Slobodians realized that with a phone and a business card, Dr. Guyula Patko wasn't simply another ordinary citizen one might encounter in that city.

"Why are you doing all this to help us?" Peter asked.

The man replied, "I have been in Belgium, Germany, and other countries. People there helped me."

Peter suggested that they summon a taxi. "No, taxi is very expensive. We will take the bus."

So the helpful stranger assisted them with their baggage, and all three rode by bus to a hotel. The woman working the check-in desk at the hotel refused to let them check in. Her objection was that this particular hotel wasn't for Americans, but only for poor Hungarians. She plainly stated, "This is not a good hotel." Instead she suggested another hotel that was a little farther.

Sensing a bargain rate, with Guyula translating, Peter explained to the lady that they were not wealthy and that any room she could offer would be fine. Nevertheless, she still insisted that he examine the room first. Only then would she register them to stay. While Sam guarded the luggage in the lobby, Peter and Guyula mounted the stairs to inspect the room. At that point, Sam shares, he had no doubts that this was the hotel they would stay in. After all, when traveling without their wives, Peter and Sam had spent many a night in the very cheapest of hotels, not to mention overnighting in train stations and airports in order to save money. (One of their favorite stories was that of staying at the "Hee Haw Motel" in Tennessee for $9.95.) However, to Sam's utter surprise, Peter descended the stairs in full agreement with the woman. "Yes," he said. "She's right. This is *not* a good hotel." They quickly decided to proceed to the better hotel she had recommended.

This time, now that their new Hungarian friend had experience with their cumbersome luggage, he telephoned for a taxi to carry them to the next hotel. Surprisingly, when the taxi arrived, the driver refused to let them into his vehicle. Why not? Because they were Americans! "They can just walk," he told their new friend. Then the driver brusquely re-entered the taxi and drove away, leaving them standing there on the sidewalk.

Eventually, they found a more agreeable taxi driver who ended up spending the evening with them finding the address of the contact after getting checked into the hotel. Finding the correct address wasn't easy, and at one point involved the taxi driver going inside a police station to get more information about the street they were looking for. Once Sam and Peter arrived at the address of their contact, it was time to thank the Hungarian man who had helped them so much. During the entire time they hadn't dared tell him the details of who they were and what they were doing in this city. During those travels Sam carried along some American magazines. These made wonderful gifts as people in Soviet-dominated areas loved to receive such magazines and to see pictures of American cars and other products. They would pass the magazines around among friends and used them to spark interesting conversations. Therefore Sam reached into his briefcase and presented Guyula with a gift of several American magazines. Sam couldn't help but notice that one of them was a *Reader's Digest* that included a feature article concerning what really happened during the Hungarian Revolution. Had he known before leaving the U.S. that he and his father would end up traveling in Hungary, he no doubt wouldn't have brought that particular issue, which would have been considered subversive literature from the Hungarian government's perspective.

Despite Guyula's pleasure at receiving this gift, his immediate response was, "Thank you very much! But...you are from America..." Then, lowering his head and whispering, he asked, "Don't you have any spiritual literature?" He wanted a Bible! Somehow he knew that in the West, people had access to the Word of God. He was hoping that these Americans would possibly have a precious copy with them. Sam and Peter were quite moved as they saw in this man's face a deep hunger for the Word of God.

The Slobodians were heavily loaded with Russian Bibles, but they had none in Hungarian. However, Sam did have a brand-new leather bound English Bible and was glad to give it to their Hungarian friend. As Sam opened it up and began to show him God's plan of salvation, at one point Sam pulled out an ink pen in order to circle a verse. But Guyula abruptly stopped his hand and said, "Please don't write. *My* Bible." It was clear how highly the man prized this gift. Seeing how God worked in this man's life to prepare safe passage for them, and at the same time seeing God use them to bring him the Gospel he so gladly received, was a great encouragement to the Slobodians in the difficult work they had undertaken of getting the God's Word behind the Iron Curtain.

A few weeks after returning to the U.S., Sam received from Guyula a thank-you note, which simply expressed thanks for the gift, but without mentioning the word "Bible." He wrote, "Thank you for your precious present. I read it every day, and reading it gives me great joy."

The Slobodians once again rejoiced and recalled the words of Jeremiah 15:16, where the prophet described his joy at finally having the Word of God, *"Thy words were found, and I did eat them; and thy word was unto me the joy and rejoicing of mine heart."*

Meanwhile, in Hungary the Slobodians went on to meet their contact, who proved to be a successful conduit for moving Bibles into Russia. In fact, at that same time there were a couple other missionaries visiting who needed Romanian literature, which the Slobodians happened to have in their suitcases. Peter and Sam gave them the Gospels and Christian literature that they had in the Romanian language. In turn, because Peter and Sam were headed for Czechoslovakia and Poland, those men supplied them with what they had in Czech and Polish languages. They went their separate ways after having encouraged and helped one another.

Though BIEM's ministry focused mainly on missionary radio, the Slobodians also engaged in smuggling Bibles into Russia on three different levels. First, they themselves served as couriers on each trip they took to the Soviet Union. Second, they provided Bibles for contacts in neighboring Soviet bloc countries. Third, they provided funds for the underground pipeline, which supplied unregistered Baptist churches with Bibles inside the Soviet Union. This was very secretive work, with as little information as possible given out. For example, when the Slobodians made a commitment in Russia with a trusted believer from the underground church, a pencil was broken. The Slobodians were given one half of the pencil and told,

Peter and Sam Slobodian standing in the customs line loaded down with Bibles and Gospel literature.

"when you are back in America and someone presents you with the other half of this pencil, then you will know that you can trust this man with funds that will be used in providing Bibles for persecuted churches in Russia."

Thus, when it came to getting Bibles into Russia or aiding the underground press, only absolutely necessary information was exchanged. What may be a surprise to Americans was that the services of the "underground" (or "unregistered," meaning they had no official status in the eyes of the authorities) churches were not that secretive. Quite often authorities knew where the Christians were meeting. The term "underground" referred more to the illegal nature of these meetings than their secrecy. However, anything to do with Bible literature, youth work, or children's ministries was highly secretive. Being caught participating in these types of activities almost always spelled immediate imprisonment, whereas attending unauthorized church services more often resulted in fines and other forms of persecution for first-time offenders.

Preaching in a Hungarian church

The following morning was Sunday, and Peter and Sam wanted to visit two churches, so their new Hungarian friend and his wife took Sam to one of the churches, and their daughter, who spoke English, led Peter to the other one. Peter didn't know it was happening, but this girl informed the pastor that Peter spoke "all languages, except Hungarian." So the pastor decided he would let Peter preach and found a man who agreed to interpret—if Peter would kindly preach in German!

Of course, not understanding Hungarian, Peter didn't realize that such plans were being arranged for him. Then, after preaching a short sermon, the pastor called Peter's name and motioned for him to approach the pulpit and preach in German so his church member could interpret Peter's German sermon into Hungarian. Taken aback, Peter explained to the young lady in English that he didn't understand German, but that he could preach in English, Spanish, Polish, or Russian. When the pastor learned that Peter understood Russian, he asked him to preach in that tongue. So Peter preached in Russian, and the pastor interpreted into Hungarian.

From Hungary, father and son proceeded to Czechoslovakia and Poland, where they gave out quite a number of Bibles as well as other literature. In Poland they were also able to share the Gospel with some of Peter's relatives. From Poland they flew back to the United States, tired from the extensive trip, but praising the Lord for the opportunities to spread His Word and to partake in His spiritual harvest.

CHAPTER 8
BIEM's Radio Ministry

For most preachers, the most satisfying form of preaching is face to face with a group of people. When a servant of God actually sees the people with whom he is sharing God's Holy Word, he will see some people nodding in agreement. He might occasionally hear a word of affirmation. He will also see faces of sinners who, hearing the truth, are obviously gripped in a spiritual struggle and for the sake of such souls the preacher will pour out his heart all the more fervently as he urges the unrepentant to renounce sin and to the Savior.

In the recording studio, Sam and Peter formed a father-son team. Sam recorded and edited the sermons that Peter preached in Russian and Ukrainian for his native land.

However, in a radio ministry, not one of those visual experiences is possible. Certainly, the radio preacher can imagine listeners out there tuning in to his sermon, but he doesn't enjoy the same speaker-listener dynamics that occur inside a church.

Peter, too, longed to preach in his homeland and to interact with perishing sinners face-to-face. Politics, however, made that dream impossible to pursue—at least in the early 1980s. But simply telling about Peter's passion for such a ministry in a historical way could never give a reader the full sense of how urgently Peter felt about preaching to his homeland. Here are his own words, as he appealed to early supporters of BIEM: [8]

The Challenge of Preaching by Radio

by Dr. Peter Slobodian

> The most effective means of reaching the lost behind the Iron Curtain is the shortwave radio. In fact, when a reporter returning from the Soviet Union was asked to name the most popular form of recreation he replied, "Church and shortwave radio." BIEM is one of the few mission agencies that is able to accept this great challenge of the twentieth century. It is a dream-come-true as we are now preaching on shortwave in the Russian language and will soon add our other native languages that are spoken in communist-held countries. During our recent trip to the Soviet Union we met many believers who had been saved as a result of the radio ministry or had first been introduced to the gospel by a radio program. In one church a new convert told of the emptiness in his life and how he listened to the radio to hear if this gospel had the answer. He soon was saved and began on his own to look for a church to attend. Now he is a regular member of a church we visited.

---

8 The source publication for this article, the *Baptist International Challenger*, became BIEM's primary newsletter. To this day, the *Challenger* (as it's called in short form) is printed four times per year to present the successes and needs of the mission fields and to challenge readers before the Lord to take a stand to promote the Gospel.

The Soviets do attempt to jam the airwaves, but this is mostly directed toward non- religious broadcasts, particularly the news media. Religious broadcasts do get through, and recently we received our first correspondence from the Soviet Union, so we know that our message is being heard. The gospel can penetrate iron curtains and iron hearts! Recently the Russian magazine *Science and Religion* blamed Soviet educators in communist countries for not being thorough enough to liquidate the desire for religion among Soviet people. The people instead are listening to shortwave radio for a clear, unbiased presentation of the hope of the gospel. Many people are becoming increasingly disillusioned with communist propaganda and want to return to the roots of their religious heritage. We must act now to give them the truth of the gospel they so greatly desire.

We challenge you to share our burden to get the gospel to millions in the Soviet Union while we still have time. Bear in mind that all Soviet citizens depend on shortwave radios to know what is happening in the free world and in the Soviet Union itself. The news in the Soviet Union is completely controlled by the government, and of course they get only what the government wants them to know. Why not give them the "good news" by the only means available—radio waves?

The Iron Curtain isn't strong enough to block out the gospel of Jesus Christ! There are thousands of deprived, persecuted men, women, and children who need our encouragement. They endure so much compared with what it costs us to broadcast there. Often upon penalty of death, imprisonment, and horrible torture, they refuse to give up their faith in the Lord Jesus Christ. They are willing to suffer anything for Christ's sake. Most Americans cannot even conceive of the extent and the severity of the persecution that is taking place in the communist-controlled countries. Yet because of the dedication of believers behind the Iron Curtain and of those in the free world, the gospel can be preached there.

We ought to be witnessing unto the Lord both in our "Jerusalem" and "in all Judea" and in "Samaria" and unto "the uttermost part of the earth" (Acts 1:8b). Should we be excused for not preaching to millions under Communism? NOT AT ALL! We should do our utmost to free as many as we can from the bondage of sin. We ought to do our job of preaching now, while there is time. We challenge you to help us put the gospel there by praying for this ministry and by your financial support. Let us not close our eyes before such a multitude of people who respond to the gospel in spite of such severe persecution. Let us obey the Great Commission wholeheartedly and fully—"Go ye into all the world" includes the millions behind the Iron Curtain. Souls will be saved and churches established even by radio as we preach the "whole counsel of God." If we are neglectful, nothing will be done, and souls will perish. What will our answer be before the judgment seat of Christ?

The believers in the Soviet Union openly prayed for radio ministry. We heard, "God bless the radio programs" many times in every church we had the opportunity to attend. This means programs from the West: of course they do not have their own. At this point we buy radio time from shortwave radio stations, but we look forward to having our own radio station. That will give us the best time and as many programs as we want. The pastors we met in the Soviet Union begged us to have Bible courses by radio in doctrine, theology, history, and even missions. They do not have such privileges as we have in the USA. They are self-educated in Bible, and they count it a great blessing if they can have at least a Bible. They cannot even imagine

> what it is like to have Bible colleges and seminaries, and yet they witness and preach at any cost. Many of us enjoy Christian radio programs daily, and there are thousands of them in the USA. Surely we can afford to have at least a few behind the Iron Curtain. Please pray for us and for this unique ministry the Lord has given us. Without your help we cannot accomplish much. If you are not able to give much, please pray that the Lord will lay this vision and burden on someone who can give. We have no other place or source to go to for help—to the Lord first, and then to His people like you. Please join us in this challenge before us. Let us hear from you soon!
>
> "Also I heard the voice of the Lord saying, whom shall I send, and who will go for us? Then said I, Here am I, send me" (Isaiah 6:8).
>
> (*Baptist International Challenger*, Vol. 2, No. 2, 1984)

However, regardless of Peter's passion, various individuals questioned BIEM's approach to evangelizing communist Europe. Not that the people who voiced their doubts didn't have compassion on lost souls. But because the historic method of preaching and establishing new churches was by gathering listeners into one geographic location and then opening the Word of God to preach face-to-face, some wondered whether the apostles or Jesus Himself would view radio waves as a viable method of evangelizing. In a subsequent issue of the *Challenger*, Sam Slobodian addressed that question in the following article:

Is Using Shortwave Radio Biblical?

by Sam Slobodian

> Ever since the radio was invented some have questioned the Scriptural authority of its use for preaching the Word of

God. In fact, in the early days of radio there were a number of God-fearing, Bible-believing preachers that condemned the radio as satanic, referring to the description of Satan in Ephesians as the "prince of the power of the air."

While those voices have for the most part been silenced by the light of common sense, there are still those who question the use of the radio as a valid missionary outreach. The point is made that since neither Christ nor the Apostle Paul used the radio, preaching by radio is not a valid New Testament missionary method.

Is there an answer to the question, "If our beloved Jesus or the great missionary Apostle Paul were walking our earth today, would they use radio?" I believe that the answer would be a resounding "Yes!" It is abundantly clear from Scriptures that Christ and the Apostle Paul used all of the means available at the time to share the Gospel. At the well and at the market place, from house to house, and from synagogue to Mars Hill, in court and in jail, in season and out of season, they practiced the admonition given to us, "Preach the Word!"

If the Apostle Paul recognized the market place, the synagogue, and Mars Hill as appropriate forums for preaching the Word of God, it is hard to imagine that he would have ignored the radio waves had they been available. In addition, today we are not using shortwave radio broadcasts as only one of many ways to preach the Word of God in the Soviet Union. Rather, we are using shortwave radio broadcasts as the only available means we in the free world currently have to preach the Gospel in countries that are closed to conventional missionary work. To ignore this method is to effectively ignore the plain command of Scripture to "go into all the world and preach the Gospel."

With over one billion shortwave radio sets in use in the world today, and with most of them in countries where information is restricted, I do not believe that our Savior or the Apostle Paul are offended that we are preaching to the one third of the world under Communism by shortwave radio. Rather, they are offended that we are not doing more. We fundamental Baptists will one day have to stand before the Lord and give an answer for not doing more to reach the communist world with the Gospel while Radio Vatican, the New Evangelicals, and the Charismatics are logging hundreds of hours weekly on international shortwave radio. Brethren, let us examine ourselves in light of Christ's command and our opportunities, and let us resolve to do more. (*Baptist International Challenger,* Vol. 4, No. 4, 1986)

However, as might be expected, Christians then living behind the Iron Curtain showed absolutely no doubt concerning the value of radio as a means of sharing God's Word. When such a ministry was still only an idea in Peter Slobodian's mind, they greatly encouraged him to proceed.

One question that was raised in the West concerning this kind of ministry was what the Soviet authorities did to block those broadcasts. During those times, the Soviet Union invested heavily in "jamming" broadcasts from the free world. Meanwhile, they broadcast Radio Moscow in 88 languages throughout the world, bombarding the air waves with clear and powerful signals. This issue was addressed by the Slobodians in the following article published in the *Challenger.*

Jamming and the Religious Broadcaster

by Sam Slobodian

In their endless effort to blind their citizens to truth, Soviet authorities often jam broadcasts from the free world. They do this by putting out electronic noise on the same frequencies as the targeted broadcasts in order to drown out those signals. The Soviets continue to do this despite protests from the free world that jamming violates such international agreements as the 1975 Helsinki Accords, the UN Universal Declaration of Human Rights, and the 1973 International Telecommunications Convention. In fact, some experts believe that the Soviet Union spends more money jamming than the entire free world spends on broadcasting!

What effect does jamming have on the religious broadcaster? Well, certain aspects of this seemingly bleak situation actually encourage us at BIEM to continue with our regular shortwave radio broadcasts. The major targets of Soviet jamming are *politically* oriented operations such as Voice of America and Radio Free Europe. In order to combat the interference, these major operations often broadcast their programs on many frequencies on different broadcast bands so that the listener can eventually find the program he wants by turning the dial. This frequent dial turning actually *helps* the religious broadcaster. Although religious broadcasters cannot afford to be on as many frequencies as the government supported operations, their stations are often picked up by the many people turning their dials. Thus jamming is a situation in which the Soviets "meant it for evil but God meant it for good."

The Word of God does not return void. There are over one billion shortwave radio sets in use today, most of them in the one-third of the world under Communism. Those radios represent the tremendous opportunity we have to meet a great need—the need that millions of listeners have of hearing the Gospel and accepting Christ. With your help we could put more programs on more stations, and more people behind the Iron Curtain would be able to hear the Word of God.

During the decades when the Soviet authorities were persecuting active Christians, believers were afraid to write letters to overseas ministries. At a time when the Soviet authorities restricted or monitored its citizens' contacts with the outside world, anyone who penned such a letter could create unnecessary hardships for himself. Nevertheless, BIEM did receive limited numbers of notes and greeting cards from people who wanted to let the Baptist International Evangelistic Ministries staff know that they were listening.

Then on March 11, 1985, Mikhail Gorbachev became General Secretary of the Communist Party in the USSR, a position that made him the political ruler of that nation. In an effort to rejuvenate his country, Gorbachev soon announced new policies called *Glasnost* ("Openness") and *Perestroika* ("Restructuring"). The Soviets stopped arresting and imprisoning Christians. (Within a few short years the Berlin Wall was dismantled, and the politics of Eastern Europe underwent rapid changes. Suddenly thousands of letters bearing Soviet postage stamps flowed into BIEM. The notes and cards from all corners of the USSR provided abundant testimony that people were indeed listening to "The Scripture Saith" on their shortwave sets.

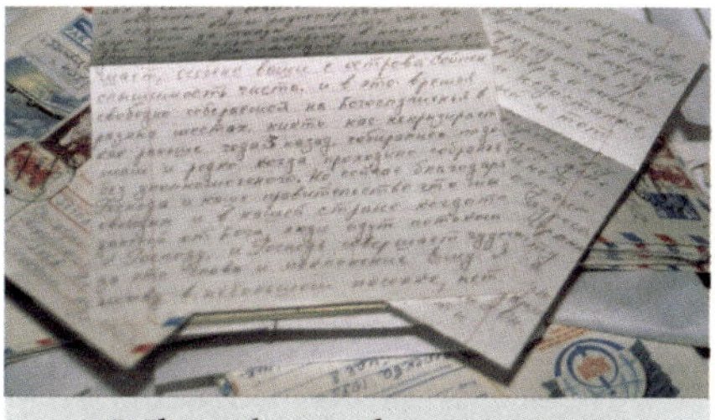
When the mail restrictions lifted, BIEM was inundated with thousands of letters from listeners.

(*Baptist International Challenger,* Vol.5, No. 2, 1987)

Some listeners asked for a New Testament, and others simply wanted to share how much they enjoyed listening to "The Scripture Saith" over their radios. What a heart-warming verification that people—both Christians and non-believers—were listening and considering the truths of God's Word as Peter shared them over the airwaves! When the Soviet Union revised its postal regulations to permit Bibles, BIEM joyfully launched a program to mail copies of God's Word in Russian to individuals who requested it.

Following are a few samples of the letters that BIEM received from listeners overseas:

From Moscow

...We thank you very much for your programs. Listening to them, I became a believer. I pray for you, and I ask the Lord to bless your labor in the vineyard of the Lord. Every evening I invite neighbors and friends, and we listen to your broadcasts on the radio. If you have the opportunity, please send us spiritual literature in the Russian language. I would like very much to have "Collection of Spiritual Hymns...."

From Smolensk

...We thank God with all our hearts for the marvelous opportunity to hear Gospel programs by radio and for this opportunity to write you this letter. My wife and I were raised in Christian families where, when Christian radio programs started, the whole family sat in a circle around the radio; all work was set aside. And up to this time we have been listening with joy to the voice of the Gospel message on the airwaves, only now in our own small room together with our four children...."

From Voroshilovgrad

"In regard to me, Christ saved me and gave me new life (before my redemption this seemed to me just words, but now—it is a fact). God reveals Himself in the soul of man with an indescribable light and gives joy, peace, and happiness....

"And I like the content in your broadcast 'The Scripture Saith' very much, the Old Testament (its symbols and rituals) and New Testament history. One begins to understand better the meaning of the two big parts of the Bible; suddenly one begins to see the deeper hidden treasures which are hidden from one's carnal vision. These are very interesting revelations…."

From Tbilisi

"I greet you with the love of our Lord Jesus Christ, dear laborers in God's vineyard! Peace unto you!

"I want to thank you for your marvelous Christian broadcasts, which are a source of spiritual food for me. This is the second year I have been listening to your broadcasts. Through these broadcasts and hearing about Christ, I felt a hunger to come to God. All of our family started to attend the evangelical Christian-Baptists' house of prayer [church]. We started to grow spiritually. I thank our Lord Jesus Christ who helped me sort of accidentally to turn my radio to your broadcasts in January of 1990. And since then God is in my heart constantly. Our daughter is studying at a Sunday school for children. On June 2 she passed a test and came out outstanding for one year of study in this school. Praise and gratitude be to our Lord and Savior Jesus Christ for His love to us!

"Esteemed Pyotr Antonovich! I pray the Lord to bless the way of this my letter. It would be a delight to receive an answer, and if it is possible, any spiritual literature for us and our daughter. She will soon be 10 years old. We would be very grateful to you."

From Ulyanovsk

"…I would like to let you know that I am an unbeliever, and my parents were the children of believing parents but never believed in God. I and my two brothers are also unbelievers, but the soul seeks God. That is why I turn to you; help us get to know the truth of God. If you can, send us a Bible and other spiritual literature. And pray for us, that God would reveal Himself to us and be our Savior and save us and our parents also, who heard so much about God. They sing the hymns which they heard while children, but they are lost sinners...."

From Moscow

"Good day, highly esteemed Pyotr Antonovich!

"Allow me to express to you and to your co-laborers in your broadcasting my great gratitude for that good and

Debbie and Mary packing Bibles and Gospel literature in response to overwhelming numbers of requests in letters.

important work which you are doing. Such broadcasts in particular are needed for people and are indispensable for people like me who have just stepped into the way of truth.

"My life's calling is to serve science. Science and religion are indivisibly tied to each other; they are the main moving power of human existence. The way to the Lord for an unbelieving man is not very easy. It was very hard for me, a man with atheistic views, to turn from the way leading to perdition to the way leading to light. Even on this road it wasn't easy to continue my way. Many different obstacles force a man to return to the foot of the mountain of light. And then one must find in himself strength to get up on his feet and start climbing again. Such falls can be expected more than once.

"Right now my climbing has reached the moment when the longest part of the way has been walked, and the end is already near. Nevertheless this small part of the long road appears most complicated. And may the Lord help me to overcome it.

"Esteemed Pyotr Antonovich, if it is not too much trouble, help me please in the final strength. In our country it is hard to get the Holy Scriptures and other spiritual literature, which are so indispensable to people who have just stepped onto the way of faith.

"Please help, if you have the opportunity; send the indispensable literature.

"I thank you very much."

From Zagorsk

"In the name of the Father, and Son, and Holy Ghost!

"Good day, esteemed Pyotr Antonovich!

"I heard your message 'Believers and unbelievers,' April 12, 1989, on the radio program "The Scripture Saith" on the 31 meter band.

"Your piercing word turned my soul upside down; it forced me to fear my own unbelief, and you guided me with your lips to the way of the Lord.

"I adjure you, my instructor, to show me the way to comprehend the teachings of our God.

"May God bless you!"

From Maladansk

"Hello, esteemed Pyotr Slobodian.

"I am your listener from the Soviet Union. I am so happy for you that all is well with you, and I bow my head before you and before that ministry which you carry out for the good of all the believers in the Soviet Union. I am 27 years old, and I did not believe before that God exists, but through the years wisdom came to me, and I understood that salvation is only in Him, in our great Lord. Your merit is in this, dear friend, that I take my needed information from your broadcasts, and God gave me salvation, and I understood that it is far better to go through this life if the Lord is with you. I now have new life. I became truly happy. I am grateful for your broadcasts. I listen to them holding my breath because so far I have no education in theology. All this need is met by your care for us believers in Russia...."

Sometimes, listeners asked the workers at BIEM to pray for them. Sample prayer requests include the following:

From Tagara

"...I live in a village where there is no church, not even another believer. I need your prayers for me and for the village that I live in, that the Lord might send revival among the people I live with...."

From Nevinnomisek

"...I have a need for your prayer also—pray for me that the Lord will give me strength to grow in His truth, and the desire of my heart for you is to pray for my daughter. Satan has bound all her mind and heart. Every day her heart is more rebellious...."

From Pavlodar

"...I have a sick daughter. She is 35; she is like a child. She does not go out. She finished 5th grade, can only read....

> Pray for us and for our children and for Irene...she believes in God and reads the literature every day."

The tone of such letters was generally not only friendly, but one of respect and sometimes even family-like relationship. Indeed, among members of the family of God there not only can be, but should be, a feeling of togetherness despite borders. This is the sense of oneness in Christ, and even those letter-writers who affirmed coming to faith in God through the radio sermons felt that principle in their lives.

How would all these individuals have responded if someone were to suggest that radio wasn't a suitable method for Christian preachers? The notion probably would have appalled them. After all, radio gave many of them their only access to Scriptural instruction.

On the other hand, the atheistic authorities who then ruled the Soviet Union probably felt otherwise. For years they had been struggling to keep religion under the thumb of state control, so quite likely they would have agreed that Russian radio sermons were not at all necessary!

Why was it that so many Soviet citizens in such far-flung regions of that enormous country were tuning in to shortwave radio broadcasts from foreign nations? After all, if you are a typical American, most likely you cannot recall the last time that you sat down and listened to an overseas shortwave broadcast. Very possibly, you have never once considered doing so in your life! So how and why were Soviet citizens tuning in "The Scripture Saith" by shortwave? BIEM's Program Director, who was Sam Slobodian in the 1980s, wrote a concise article for other Americans who wondered the same things.

Here is that article, titled "Vast Communist Shortwave Audience No Surprise."

Vast Communist Shortwave Audience No Surprise

by Sam Slobodian

In the United States most people not only do not have a shortwave radio, but rarely even know someone who does. This is because most who listen to shortwave radio in our country are hobbyists and represent a very small portion of the American public. As a result when people in the United States are informed of the huge multitudes of shortwave radio listeners in other parts of the world they are often surprised.

In light of the circumstances that exist in a communist country we should not be surprised that so many are listening to international shortwave radio broadcasts from the free world. In fact, when a country's press and electronic media are strongly controlled by a communist government we should expect large numbers of people to listen to the single source of reliable and unrestricted radio broadcasts from the free world. While in the United States almost every home has a television, in communist countries like the Soviet Union almost every home has a shortwave radio set. It would be just as difficult to find a home in our country without a television set as it would be to find a home in Russia and many other communist countries without a shortwave radio. Furthermore, If shortwave were the only way we in America could find out what is going on in our own country and around the world, we would all have shortwave radio sets too. And so it should come as no surprise to read statements in *Reader's Digest* that there are over one billion shortwave radio sets in use in the world today or to read in *USA Today* that there are over 100 million listeners of just the *Voice of America* over shortwave radio. Most of this vast audience is, of course, composed of people in communist countries who are eager to listen to the only available source of reliable information that they can obtain.

The availability of shortwave radio sets in communist countries is not a problem; otherwise, such a huge audience couldn't exist. We have personally been in five communist countries, and in each one we saw firsthand that shortwave radios were readily available for purchase. We will address the reasons the communist governments allow this availability in a future article. There can be no doubt that even communist government officials of all ranks themselves listen to broadcasts from the free world. God's people here in America must realize that we have a great opportunity to reach people in communist countries for Christ. While they are turning to their shortwave radio sets to find some news, let us tell them the best news. Let us tell them the good news of the Gospel. As we have said before, at BIEM it is our calling and our privilege to preach the story of our blessed Savior to the homes and hearts of many listeners in countries closed to conventional missionary work. As we hear the response of those who have heard, two facts stand out. One is the fact of the tremendous power of God that pierces even hearts schooled from childhood in the atheistic stronghold of Communism. Second, we are deeply pressed with the need to do much more. Please pray with us for the necessary funds that we need for our broadcasts so that more who cannot hear any other way will hear the Word of God through our shortwave broadcasts.

(*Baptist International Challenger,* Vol. 6, No. 1, 1988)

The Scope of BIEM's Radio Ministry

Eventually BIEM was able to broadcast Peter's preaching in Russian and Ukrainian via seven different international radio stations. While some were Christian stations like HCJB and Far East Broadcasting

Company, others were simply secular stations from whom BIEM was able to purchase radio time. In negotiating contracts for these broadcasts, the Slobodians were pleased to learn that there was no limitation on what could be preached. Peter was free to preach the whole counsel of God. As one station manager explained, "You can say whatever

Peter and Mary listening to their own broadcast in the home of Pastor Fyodr Mahovitsky in Leningrad.

you want, so long as you don't advocate the violent overthrow of the American government." He went on to explain that, while they could encourage the overthrow of the American government, they couldn't advocate the "violent" overthrow of the government. Of course BIEM wasn't interested in mixing any politics at all into the messages. When it came to the preaching and programming of the radio broadcasts, Peter followed the clear pattern of the Apostle Paul when he entered Corinth, "For I determined not to know any thing among you, save Jesus Christ, and him crucified" (1 Corinthians 2:2).

CHAPTER 9

New Opportunities in Russia

Toward the end of the 1980's, the free world began to hear two particular Russian words that were embraced by the new leader of the Soviet Union, Mikhail Gorbachev. The words were *glasnost*, which means "openness" and *perestroika*, which means "restructuring."

Although the Soviet authorities had refused tourist visas for the Slobodians since 1985, Peter decided to apply again during this new age of *perestroika*. After all, even though the radio ministry was achieving its goals of evangelizing and providing spiritual nourishment to believers, Peter's heart still longed to visit personally the land of his youth. This time, the applications were accepted! So Peter, Mary, and their youngest daughter Debbie purchased airline tickets to the USSR in the autumn of 1989. In their suitcases they had packed a good number of Russian Bibles, plus some other literature. The first Soviet city on their itinerary was Moscow.

Because the simplest way to enter the Soviet Union in those days was as part of a tourist group, the three traveled with a guided tour. However, of all the Americans in the group, Peter and Mary were the only ones who could speak Russian. At that time, travelers to the Soviet Union still had no right to choose the hotel of their choice or to make their own reservations. Such decisions were all strictly controlled by the government through Intourist, the Soviet agency that coordinated tourist activity inside the USSR.

When the Slobodians arrived at Moscow's Sheremetevo Airport, Intourist assigned them to the twenty-five-story Cosmos Hotel, which had been built by a French firm in 1980. That was good news, because at that time the Cosmos was one of the newer and nicer hotels in the capital. In addition, it was conveniently located near the VDNKh subway station, which seemed to promise quick access to numerous points all over the city. However, Intourist had no intentions of encouraging independent, unescorted travel. Instead, the agency appointed its own guides to stay with the tourist group throughout the trip.

For each Soviet city that the three Americans visited, Intourist assigned a local guide to escort the travelers around and, no doubt, to keep a watchful eye on their activities. "He was a very bad person," Peter later commented about one Intourist agent who shepherded their group. "He was completely dedicated to the Communist Party. Every place we went, he would criticize the United States and always defended Communism."

In Moscow the assigned guide was a young woman who was quite educated. Peter started to give her a testimony about Christ. But she would not listen.

"I am a Communist," she stated. "And as a Communist, I do not care about a religion."

Peter replied, "I have visited many countries, and nowhere have I found a people who are more religious than in the Soviet Union."

Despite their young guide's surprised protests to the contrary, Peter maintained that Communism is a form of religion. Each day as they toured Moscow, Peter talked with her and quoted Scriptures. Eventually she relaxed a little and became friendlier. She even began asking him questions.

Because Vladimir Lenin's tomb was (and still is to this day) a major attraction for visitors to Moscow, the Slobodians decided to visit it. When they arrived at Red Square, the line of people waiting for their turn to enter was incredibly long. Literally thousands of people stood in a line that stretched out of Red Square, around a corner, and down along the street. Everyone waited to glimpse Vladimir Lenin—legendary founder of the Soviet Union—whose embalmed corpse was on display in a glass coffin inside the marble mausoleum. The Americans stepped into line with their Intourist guide and began the slow shuffle forward. When the group at last drew close to the tomb, uniformed soldiers scrutinized each person, requested to see the contents of pockets, and gave instructions of what to do and not do inside.

"No hands in your pockets," the soldiers instructed. "No talking until you exit."

Just then a man directly in front of the Slobodians whispered a comment to his companion.

A grumpy-looking soldier stepped closer and chastised the man who had whispered. "You are not to talk in this place. This is a holy place."

When Peter's group exited out the rear, he caught the eyes of the Intourist guide. "Did you hear what that guard said? He said this is a 'holy place.' What did I tell you? Communism is a religion."

This time the young woman was speechless and couldn't deny his remark. What could she say? So she simply listened.

"Have you by any chance ever read the Bible?" Peter continued.

"I read part of it, but only one time, and just a small portion. I was visiting one of my girlfriends, and I saw that she had a Bible in English. An American tourist had given it to her as a gift. But that one occasion when I was in her apartment was the only time."

"Would you like to own your own Bible?"

"After all these days of talking with you, yes, I would like to have a Bible."

He asked in what language she wanted it, and she replied that she was very good in English and that she would like an English Bible. But because she was born and living in Moscow, she told him, "A Russian Bible."

"I have a Russian Bible with me," Peter told her.

The fact was that their group possessed a good number of Russian Bibles. But because the customs workers had nearly confiscated them, he was concerned that this young government employee might denounce them for proselytizing. If she did, they might lose all their Bibles. So for the moment, he felt it would be best if she didn't know that he carried more than one on this trip.

She said, "If you have only one Bible in Russian, you keep it for yourself."

But Peter gave it to her, explaining that, when he returned to the United States, he could get as many Bibles as he wanted. She accepted it happily. Peter never knew whether that gift bore any fruit in that young Communist's life. But what he did know for sure was that the Lord had used their daily conversations to soften her heart and to open her eyes to truths she had never considered before. He had sown the seed of God's Word and prayed for the Holy Spirit to bless that effort.

Peter with Pastor Mahovitsky, who served time in Soviet prisons for his faith.

On that trip Peter was able to preach in unregistered Baptist churches in Moscow, Leningrad (now renamed St. Petersburg) in Russia, and in Kiev and Odessa in Ukraine. How was that possible on a guided tour? As members of the tour group, the Slobodians' days were filled with guided site-seeing, but then the group was deposited back at their local hotel most evenings and usually left on their own. So the three Christians simply broke completely away from the tour group on Sundays and on a couple of the weeknights. If the Intourist guides were annoyed, they never expressed it to the Slobodians. Through these meetings Peter was personally able to fellowship once again with pastors whom he had gotten to know previously as well as to establish friendships with some pastors who had still been imprisoned the last time Peter was in Russia. They were now released from the Soviet prison system, and Peter used every opportunity possible to meet and reach out to these heroes of the faith. Such meetings were a special blessing since BIEM was one of the organizations that made known the plight of Christians undergoing persecution for the faith through BIEM's publication, the *Challenger.* Therefore, after writing about the these brave pastors and Christians for years, it was a great thrill and humbling experience for the Slobodians to meet them face to face and enjoy fellowshipping with such inspiring servants of Christ.

Peter and Sam meeting with Peter Rumachik, who was imprisoned for over 18 years for faithfulness to Christ.

This was a historic trip for the Slobodians, and proved to be an uplifting and humbling experience to fellowship with Russian pastors and to preach in the unregistered churches. Shortly after their return to the United States, BIEM produced a video of their travels among those unregistered Baptist churches titled *Worship in Russia.* Following is a partial transcript from that video. (Note: in the actual video, various individuals take turns in narrating. This fact isn't clear from the printed text.)

Worship in Russia

Excerpted transcript from Worship in Russia
video produced by BIEM in 1989

In centuries past, the czars of Russia had many cathedrals built to honor the god of the Russian Orthodox religion and to display their great wealth and power. When the communists took over and atheism became the official religion of state, these buildings were used for warehouses, museums, and other institutions.

Recently, in the new spirit of *glasnost* or "openness," the Soviet state has returned some of its buildings to the people. This church is one of them. Today it houses a functional Russian Orthodox church.

And what changes has *glasnost* brought to our brothers and sisters in Christ who live in the Soviet Union? To answer this question we will take you inside the worship services of several unregistered Baptist churches. Those which the West often calls underground churches. "Illegal" is the word that Soviet authorities use. And it is actually more accurate than our term "underground." For there is nothing secretive or hidden about their meetings and activities, as you can see here. They are considered illegal because they have chosen not to register their congregations officially according to the laws of the Soviet state. They fear that doing so will allow the state to con-

Persecuted believers meeting in the forest in the dead of winter.

trol and restrict their practice of worship, even though their government in this era of openness and relative freedom promises them otherwise. They have, however, been quick to take advantage of the State's new, more tolerant, attitude toward religion, and many unregistered congregations have even gone ahead and built buildings for themselves without permits. They are simple constructions, with no more than four walls and a roof.

Turning to this man, the pastor of this church outside Leningrad, my father Dr. Peter Slobodian said, "It is quite cold; do you have heat?"

"We do not have heat."

"It is quite cold," my father said again. "Yes, my brother," said the pastor. "But it is better than in the woods."

"Did you have the Lord's supper in the woods in the winter?"

"Yes, we brought a small table, we put it in the snow, and we had the Lord's supper."

The amount of freedom that each church enjoys is largely dependent on the whims of its local authorities even today under *glasnost*. While the higher-ups in Moscow are still talking about possibly changing the anti-religion laws, Christians in many towns and villages throughout the Soviet Union are being given heavy and burdensome fines for such things as holding services in their homes. The building which this church outside Odessa meets in is the third one they have built in three years' time. The first two were demolished by the local authorities. When they threatened the destruction of this one as well, the church said they would send a delegation to Gorbachev, and so far the authorities have left this building alone.

Another problem these churches face is a serious lack of Bibles and printed materials. Notice that when this congregation sings a song based on Romans 8:38–39, the pastor first reads these verses to them because so few have Bibles with which to follow along. And how many hymnals do you see in this choir? Even the choir director's stand is empty.

We take you now to a service of an unregistered church on the outskirts of Moscow. As you can see, their building wasn't large enough to hold all the people who came on this Sunday. They stood outside listening in at the open doors and windows. Inside the building, every seat was taken and more people were standing in all the available space at the back and in the aisle. They stood there for five hours, 10 a.m. to 3 p.m. That's a long service, even by Russian standards. Usually their services are only two to three hours long, but this one was special for it was a day set aside to thank God for the harvest. There was much music throughout the service, both congregational singing and special numbers.

People of all ages take part in the services, not only by singing and playing, but also by reciting Christian poetry and Scripture verses. Children are especially encouraged to do so. There was no Sunday school or junior church for these children; they sat in the front rows for the entire service, occasionally going outside for a break. There is a great need for children's materials in the USSR. The Christian parents we met in every church begged and begged us to send them children's Bibles. Now that God has opened the door for us, we must accept the challenge to provide Soviet Christians with illustrated materials for teaching children about the Word of God.

As in every other church we visited, I was asked to preach. "Peace unto you, brothers and sisters!"

"With peace we accept you!" they stood and said.

When I gave them greetings from you in America, they stood again to accept your greetings, as is their custom. Some of them recognize my voice having heard our shortwave radio programs *The Scripture Saith*. But this was the first time many of them had seen me in person.

The Holy Spirit has greatly blessed and used my father's radio preaching in a mighty way. Not only have many been saved throughout the Soviet Union but also churches have been established as a result of our radio ministry. We have received thousands of letters, nearly all asking for Bibles. Someone from Siberia writes, "A young man started to attend our church recently who was saved through your broadcasts. He is very happy and would love to have a Bible." A soldier in Krasnodor writes, "I accepted Christ as my Savior while serving in the army. My friend had a radio, and we always found a way to listen to your preaching. One friend had a Bible we could read. I have come home now and started to witness to my parents and family. They are all against me, and I don't even have a Bible to prove to them my faith in Christ." Some of the most touching requests come from the lost seeking help in finding Christ. A man named Ganage writes, "With great joy I listen to your broadcasts and find in them many new and interesting things for myself. I am 20 years old, but it seems to me I have no future. And when I hear your radio programs, my eyes fill up with tears and it seems as if Jesus Himself turns to me and says, 'Come to me, and I will give you peace.' In such moments I want to put my life into His hands that He

Wherever Peter traveled, there were many eager to ask questions.

may become my Lord and Savior. But there is always something holding me back. I beg you please help me. And if you can, please send me a Bible and spiritual literature."

Many talked to me afterwards and asked many questions. I didn't know it, but someone taped our conversation as well as the sermon and sent them on to Odessa, the next city we would be in. By the time we got there the Christians in Odessa as you see here were prepared with even more questions to ask me. These men have not had the advantage of Bible schools or seminaries. So they were eager to learn what they could. Now that God has opened the door for us, we must accept the challenge to provide Soviet Christians with training materials for pastors and lay people.

Often several preachers will preach over the course of a typical Russia service. And sometimes they will have even more than one invitation. That is exactly what happened at this service outside Moscow. We could see the Holy Spirit working as people came forward one by one to pray aloud.

"Lord, Lord, I beg you, forgive me, Lord. Forgive all my sins I have committed. I am begging You, I am begging You, I am begging You, forgive.

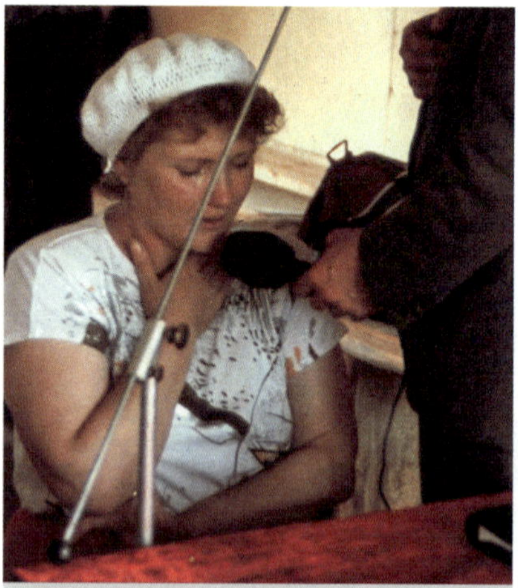

People coming forward to be saved.

Young and old, men and women, they just kept coming forward. Many said they had come to this church for the first time.

"Lord, You helped me to come here. I praise You for that and for these services. You helped me to come to know You. I praise You for everything."

You are witnessing here part of the great revival taking place in the Soviet Union, and the Word of God is the key to it. This girl was very broken-hearted and cried for a long time.

"Do you want to know the will of God?"

"Yes."

"Do you have the Word of God?"

"No. Do you want to read and go deep into the truth of God?"

"Yes."

"Let this Book forever break you away from sin. May the Lord be the dearest thing in the whole world to you."

You see and hear how important Bibles and Christian literature are to these people. This church happily displays their small supply in front. But they do not keep it for themselves. On this particular Sunday they have a whole table of New Testaments and children's Bibles. These were brought to them by tourists from the West. So the pastors were able to give something to everyone who came forward that day.

The small cards you see him reading and passing out were printed on the underground press.

The pastors prayed for everyone who came forward and then questioned and exhorted each one.

"What's your name? Do you believe the Lord forgave you? Do you want to do His will? May God help you. We will pray for you, and we want to give you the life of Christ so you can get to know Him more and more. Amen."

"Let Christ be the purpose of your life. The essence of life and the way in your further walk with the Lord. Take, please, this book."

With such a tremendous revival going, such a yearning hunger for the Word of God, they do not have nearly enough Bibles to meet the demand in their city. And those people who do not live within the reach of tourists suffer an even greater need. Listen to what one of our listeners wrote to us:

"We very much need spiritual literature Not so much for us, but those around us friends, acquaintances, relatives and loved ones. The time for evangelism is upon us. The time for revival and harvest has begun. The thirst to know the Word of God is evident, and we have no sickles for the harvest. Unbelievers beg us for spiritual literature. A New Testament, a Bible, and we have none to give them to satisfy their desire. We gave away all that we had for ourselves. We are left with almost nothing, and the thirst for the Word of God is increasing. We really grieve for them because we have nothing to give them. Dear friends we really beg you, help us with anything you can. If you are able, please send us any literature you have."

We must accept this challenge to provide them with Bibles and Christian literature.

At the end of the service the pastor gathered everyone who had come forward during the invitations together up on the platform. It was a little hard maneuvering all these people in such crowded conditions. Then members of the congregation took turns praying for these new converts.

"We ask, Lord, that they might read and that they might know You. Not only that they would get to know You but that they would tell others."

After the service, one pastor sat these people down and began a new converts class for them as soon as most of the crowd had moved outside....

Time after time, sometimes with family and sometimes with other believers, Peter booked trips, not just to the Soviet Union, but also to other lands in Eastern Europe. In July of 1990, Peter and Mary traveled with their son Sam, his wife Amy, plus three businessmen and their wives who were involved in BIEM's ministry. In their luggage this sizeable group managed to take along many boxes of Bibles, New Testaments, Bible commentaries, plus useful items that could be exchanged or sold.

This American group was warmly welcomed by Russian believers, who insisted the visitors sing as a group, which they had never done before.

This time the group flew first to Helsinki, Finland. (By this time it was possible to travel more independently, without an Intourist guide.) From there they drove to the city of Leningrad. At the border crossing, all they could do was stand by and watch as uniformed border guards opened and examined their boxes of literature.

"It is illegal to bring these things into our country," a customs agent declared. "We have to confiscate them."

When the Americans objected, the customs worker summoned a supervisor with more authority. When this man walked over, he scrutinized the cardboard cartons and said, "You cannot keep these."

"But we have many friends in the Soviet Union," Peter explained. "These are presents for our friends."

"Oh, those are gifts? You don't intend to sell them?"

"No, we won't sell them. We will only give them as free gifts to our friends."

The official stood there, scrutinizing the contents of one box. From the light in his eyes, it was clear that some new, unspoken train of thought was developing in his mind. He stopped perusing and looked Peter in the eye. "If these are really gifts, may I have one Bible as a gift?"

Peter beamed. This is exactly the kind of request that a missionary likes to hear. "Yes, you can have a gift!"

Then the man pointed at a book in another carton. "What kind of book is that?"

"That is a commentary that explains the Bible," Peter said.

"May I also have a commentary as a present?"

"Of course."

Peter watched as a female worker picked up a children's book.

"What is this?" she asked aloud.

"It's a children's Bible."

When she opened it and saw the beautiful, full-color illustrations on glossy paper inside, she exclaimed, "Oh my, how beautiful this is!"

"Do you have any grandchildren?" Peter asked.

"Yes."

"Then you may keep that book as a gift for them."

She was ecstatic. "Thank you very much!"

The customs agent who had received the Bible and commentary permitted the group to keep all of their cartons of books and to take them into the Soviet Union.

When the group arrived in Leningrad, their hotel was the same one where Peter had stayed on a previous trip. Some of the employees recognized Peter from his earlier visit (at that time American visitors who could fluently speak Russian were still relatively rare and memorable), and they saw that he had other Americans with him this time. They spread the news to their fellow workers: "Baptists from America have come to visit. Their leader is a Russian, and they brought Bibles!" The employees on duty asked the group for Bibles and other Christian literature, and of course the travelers were delighted to oblige.

The next morning the Americans took to the streets with their literature. By this time changes had begun sweeping through the USSR, and there was no longer an Intourist guide to monitor and control their activities. On the streets, Sam Slobodian would play his trumpet, and then they would preach to whatever crowd gathered to listen. Following the sermon, the Christians would distribute Bibles and New Testaments to all who wanted one. Such free gifts of Christian literature were an unheard-of novelty in this land that used to confiscate and destroy Bibles. So when people received a Bible or New Testament, they often opened it and began to read on the spot.

Peter would preach while people gathered on the streets to listen.

On Sunday morning Peter and Sam preached in an unregistered Baptist church (in other words, one that operated without the government's official permission to exist), and in the evening they distributed more literature. They also visited historical sites around Leningrad before setting out for Moscow, the capital.

In Moscow they once more checked into the Cosmos Hotel. There, too, some employees remembered Peter from his earlier stay. Once again hotel employees requested Christian literature. Although it wasn't possible to engage in actual church-planting, the travelers thanked the Lord for opportunities to sow His Word in a land steeped in atheism.

Bibles being given to the unregistered churches.

The group had many opportunities to fellowship with believers, to preach in services, and to distribute aid to needy Christians. A highlight of this trip was that, through an unusual and remarkable opportunity, the group was able to purchase a bus load of Bibles and deliver them to the unregistered Baptist churches.

Of course, neither Peter nor anyone else at BIEM in those days took these new opportunities for granted. There was a widespread concern that this new, wide-open door was merely temporary and that it would soon slam shut again. Therefore, the focus of Peter and BIEM was to work while it was yet day and to take advantage of the unprecedented opportunities to travel to and preach in the USSR. Although the radio broadcasts continued, the ministry engaged in a concerted effort to travel to the former Soviet Union to evangelize and win as many to Christ as possible before Russia could revert back to Communism as some predicted. Following is an account of one of those missionary journeys from 1990, reprinted from the *Challenger:*

Pictorial Report on December 1990 Trip to the Soviet Union

By Missionary Sam Slobodian, Program Director

Baptist International Evangelistic Ministries, or BIEM as we call it, is a mission agency reaching behind the Iron Curtain in obedience to our Savior's command to go into all the world—including the one-third of the world under Communism. Thus in September of 1990 Peter and Sam Slobodian of BIEM were contacted by a group of evangelists who had a desire to preach the Gospel in the Soviet Union. These evangelists—Tom Farrell, Mike Duffy, Neil Cadwell, and Bill Crockett—told the Slobodians of their burden to take a trip into Russia.

After they contacted us, we developed a plan under God's leading to gather a team to go to Russia in December to distribute Bibles and literature, preach evangelistically in as many services as possible, meet with pastors and church leaders, and gather information for furthering the cause of

Christ in the Soviet Union. Eventually we formed a team of 18 people, including pastors Guy Conn, Steve Dean, Pat

Group from 1990 trip to USSR.

Kappenman, James Kelly, and David Sanders. The pastors, evangelists, and BIEM missionaries were joined by Bob Brown, John Glass, Richard Miller, Wayne Sanders, Paul Troth, and Gerald Woychik. Russia was a new experience for all except Peter, Mary and Sam Slobodian, as we have often been to Russia to preach the Word of God, distribute Bibles and literature, and meet with those whom we serve.

On this trip we brought with us 47 grossly overweight pieces of baggage, 18 of which were double boxes, taped together, of Russia Bibles. With God's help we passed through customs even though only religious materials cleared through officially registered church channels are supposed to be permitted. Because we lacked the required permits, some of us had to do some skillful maneuvering and explaining, yet we all recognize that the main reason we passed through with all those materials was the power of the prayers of many who were earnestly and continually holding this project up before the Lord.

Once we were through customs and into the country, we found churches packed with people hungry for the Word of God. Many in Russia are disillusioned with Communism and have turned to Christ. What a privilege to preach the precious Gospel to thirsty souls! As the invitations were extended in the 12 services we were in, we saw over 200 receive Christ. Those saved came from every age group and many walks of life. The young soldier pictured below was the first one down the aisle in one service. The aisles would fill up and sinners would individually and publicly repent and receive Christ. Christians would deal with the folks as they came forward. Pastors and others would pray aloud for the new converts, and then after the service they would give them immediate instructions in their new life.

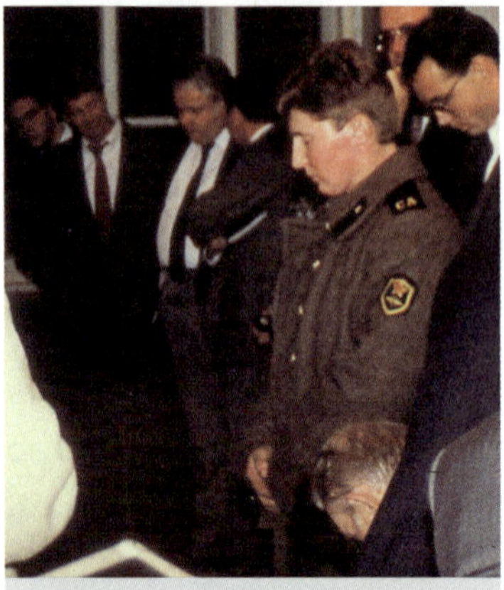

This soldier was one of the first down the aisle to be saved.

Churches meeting in homes would lay boards across chairs or stools to form make-shift pews. People would jam into every available inch of space. Once the living room filled up, the hallway, bedrooms, and kitchen would receive even more people who then stood straining to hear, soaking in the Word of God. They often stood there for hours, for Russians, in general, are not in a hurry when it comes to worship. At the invitation lost sinners would make their own aisle through the crowd as they pushed forward to receive Christ. Many of

Newly saved believers had many questions to ask.

these people who came to the evening services and received Christ had heard our team proclaim Christ in the city squares earlier that day.

We had many opportunities to fellowship with our brothers and sisters in Christ. Below is a picture we took as Pastor Naprienko's family favored us with beautiful music. Seated at the head of the table in the following picture is a pastor who had been imprisoned for a total of 15 years.

At the head of the table is Pastor Ryzhuk, who was imprisoned for many years.

We had over 2500 children's Bibles and over 15,000 Bibles shipped ahead of us. It was a great joy to hear that our brothers had received these materials and were distributing them and using them in lending libraries, which are effectively reaching many for Christ.

While there, we were able to personally give several boxes and suitcases full of Bibles and other materials to every church we visited. In addition to what had been shipped ahead of us, we brought along with us 1620 Russian and Ukrainian Bibles, 900 Russian and Ukrainian New Testaments, 500 Gospels of John, 200 other assorted books and children's materials, and 34,000 Gospel tracts. When the newly saved lady pictured below received her Bible, she hugged and kissed it repeatedly, brining many of us to tears.

There are many millions in the Soviet Union without Bibles. Some have known the Lord for many years and never owned their own Bible. When they at last get the opportunity, they hungrily reach for a Bible or any Christian literature.

Hands reaching for Gospel literature.

They also have other needs. For example, several churches are in great need of a church building. We were able to give significant contributions toward their construction projects. The believers we helped thanked us and then gave even more thanks to the Lord; some of them would shed tears of joy.

Handing out tracts in Russia was a crowd-gathering occasion. Our team passed out thousands of tracts. People stood in the cold and read every word. They asked questions and requested additional copies for their friends.

Throughout our trip, Dr. Peter Slobodian was continually meeting with pastors and church leaders who were anxious for his information, insight, and help. Churches and pastors in the Soviet Union are facing many new problems and issues today. Daily, often well into the night, they would glean all the information they could from Dr Slobodian.

During one of those sessions, the pastor in whose home we were interrupted the meeting to turn on the radio; we heard our program, *The Scripture Saith*, coming in loud and clear that very moment!

We also had the great joy of meeting some of those who had been saved as a result of our broadcasts.

Having witnessed firsthand the impact of the radio, we are convinced of the need to increase and at least double our broadcasts.

There is also a pressing need to provide training for Christians via radio and correspondence. If we Bible-believing Baptists do not teach and indoctrinate Soviet Christians, we will one day deeply regret having missed the opportunity!

Some of our team members had the opportunity to speak to students at Leningrad University and at this high school, and many students received Christ. They were willing to make their decision publicly known among their classmates.

Peter preaching in the entrance to the subway.

We started our street meetings in the subway by playing the trumpet and singing. After a crowd gathered, we began preaching.

We encountered only one heckler, who shouted, "Pray to Gorbachev!" He was quickly surrounded, however, by a mob that nearly beat him up. They have had enough of Gorbachev, Lenin and all the rest; they want to hear about JESUS.

Some of our most memorable meetings were those held in the public square across from the opera house in Lvov. This is the same spot where the city residents toppled a large statue of Lenin. Today nothing stands there in Lenin's place. We stood on one side of that empty space where the idol of Lenin had been cast down, and we gathered a large crowed with trumpet playing and singing. Crowds gathered and grew. Dr. Slobodian and the evangelists preached, and they

People gathered as Sam played on the trumpet.

preached with power. Despite the frigid cold of the Ukrainian December, the people stood, listened, and responded—some with tears in their eyes. Many turned to Christ as the Word of God was held up and the Gospel preached. Workers from local churches dealt with those who responded and collected their names and addresses.

Peter preaching to a crowd that gathered on
a place where Lenin once stood.

The rest of our team moved to the other side of the square, where once again we began with music and then preached the Word. The crowd at the second meeting was just as attentive and receptive as the first had been.

We then moved to yet a third location. Once again a large crowd formed, and many, many responded to the

People raising hands for salvation.

Gospel. Everyone on our team was profoundly affected by the amazing receptivity and hunger they witnessed. People thanked us profusely, some with many tears. When we had to leave, many remained standing there as if they were waiting to hear more. It was as if they expected someone else to come. One time as our team, frozen and numbed by the cold, climbed back into the bus, one said, "My feet are cold, but my heart is warm."

So great was the impact of the Gospel meetings that the Soviet media came out to cover our street meetings. The next day journalists from the city's two leading newspapers came to our hotel and interviewed Peter Slobodian for almost two hours. In this manner the Lord allowed our message to reach the printed page also.

Are the people of the Soviet Union receptive to the Gospel? YES, THEY ARE. Is there opportunity to reach them effectively today? YES—LIKE NEVER BEFORE. Will Bible-believing Christians and churches in the United States do their part in the battle for the Soviet souls? WE MUST!

Peter being interviewed by the media.

But it may mean doing MORE. On our flight from New York to the USSR we met nearly 200 young Russians returning home after their third Moonie indoctrination seminar. One of our hotels in the Soviet Union was full of Seventh Day Adventists mapping strategies and launching their efforts in the Soviet Union. There is a hopelessness and a void in the lives of Russian people today. They are searching and open. We must reach them for Christ and teach them the Bible. As we at Baptist International expand our efforts into the Soviet Union, we need your help. Will you pray and will you give so that these people have an opportunity to hear a Bible message and receive Christ?

As the reforms introduced by *glasnost* and *perestroika* continued to pave the way for dramatic changes in Russia, the old Soviet Union disintegrated, and by the end of December 1991, the red Soviet flag over the Kremlin was lowered for the last time, and the Union of Soviet Socialist Republics passed into history. In its place, the fifteen former Soviet republics became new, separate nations, such as Ukraine, Georgia, Belarus, Russia, etc. This turn of events provided new opportunities for the Slobodians and BIEM. For example, the lifting of mail restrictions begun in the late 1980s resulted in a remarkable increase in the amount of mail BIEM received in response to Peter's preaching.

BIEM's office was flooded with thousands of letters from all eleven times zones of the lands that had been the USSR.

Furthermore this openness of the mail system enabled BIEM to write back to listeners. Even better, it made it possible for BIEM to mail Bibles and Christian literature to a land that was starving for the Word of God. With the help of churches and individual supporters, BIEM mobilized to send thousands upon thousands of packets containing Bibles and literature to those listeners requesting them. Russian Bible printing projects were launched, and before long BIEM was even able to send massive container shipments of Bibles to Russia.

Peter and everyone else at BIEM rejoiced along with the free world, which watched as the Iron Curtain crashed down and crowds toppled statues of Lenin all over those lands. Almost overnight, religious freedom was introduced to Russia to such a degree that not only were Americans allowed to preach in public places, but they were encouraged to do so and drew crowds of hungry listeners. When it became evident that one could even preach the Word of God in public schools, it suddenly seemed that—at least for the moment—Russia actually permitted more freedom for evangelism than did the United States!

Crowds of hungry listeners.

CHAPTER 10

Church Planting in Russia & Eastern Europe

In retrospect, three different phases of ministry emerged as Peter and everyone with BIEM concentrated on the goal of reaching Russia and Eastern Europe for Christ.

The first phase was missionary radio, accomplished by producing Gospel-preaching programs in Russian and Ukrainian and airing them throughout the Soviet Union by international shortwave radio. Of course, during the early years of BIEM, the ministry also engaged in smuggling Bibles, aiding persecuted Christians, and publicizing the plight of suffering Christians behind the Iron Curtain. However, Peter and BIEM conducted all of those activities with limitations. But shortwave radio had no limitation and was clearly the door widest open for missionary work in those restricted countries. Therefore, BIEM's first phase of ministry concentrated primarily on Peter's radio preaching.

Peter preaching at a large evangelistic meeting in Moldova.

The second phase of ministry was the result of new opportunities that emerged from the reforms that came about through *glasnost* and *perestroika*. As Peter and BIEM launched into on-location evangelism and Bible distribution in response to the great spiritual hunger and newly opened freedoms, this period featured mission trips overseas. Many evangelistic campaigns were held, often connected with Bible distribution. Naturally, in each city these evangelistic meetings were coordinated with local churches, which would engage in follow-up efforts after the meetings were over.

Receiving flowers presented by the organizers of the evangelistic campaign.

This second phase of BIEM's ministry and its focus on on-the-spot evangelism formed a transitional period, which coincided perfectly with an unprecedented hunger for spiritual truth. One survey done during those times indicated that 83% of the citizens in those lands were searching for a new belief system! As one Russian man stated, "For 70 years we were told that there was no God and that Communism would prevail over capitalism. Now, since we have seen that it is capitalism which has prevailed while Communism failed, we now suspect that our government was wrong about God as well." During those times people would crowd into any place where the Bible was being preached. Just passing out tracts or any spiritual literature would draw a huge crowd.

Peter speaking to a spiritually hungry crowd.

Such enthusiastic receptivity was unparalleled, and it was no surprise when studies conducted by social scientists later indicated that during that period, the largest-ever swing in a nation's belief structure occurred in Russia. However, mission experts understood that such a mood when so many people were flocking to hear the Word wasn't going to last.

Furthermore, most people who were familiar with the history and politics of the region doubted that the wide-open religious freedom would last. An abrupt return to a totalitarian state wasn't hard to imagine. However, as time passed, it became clear that at least many of the new freedoms were going to remain. After a hard-liner coup was squelched by Boris Yeltsin, who ended up dismantling a parliament that was resisting the country's direction toward democracy and reform, it seemed that the old Soviet Union was gone for good.

As the reality of formerly Communistic countries now being open for conventional missionary work set in, Peter and BIEM assessed what direction BIEM should take in response to the fact that the field conditions of the countries they were targeting had changed so dramatically. When Peter founded BIEM, the mission targeted countries that were closed to conventional missionary work. There were numerous limitations. The best avenue for evangelistic work had clearly been to broadcast international shortwave Gospel radio programs into the Soviet Union. Now, however, countless new opportunities had sprung up. Just about any kind of ministry that could be envisioned could also now be executed without interference from a hostile government.

In light of the completely altered conditions on the field and the wide variety of new avenues through which missionary work could be performed, inevitable question arose for Peter and BIEM: what should BIEM do now? How should the ministry respond to the changes? What would be the best way to channel the mission's resources towards Russia and Eastern Europe? Since the door was now open for traditional residential missionaries to live and operate in country, should BIEM move its operation from the U.S. to Russia?

As BIEM's future was prayerfully being discussed at a BIEM board of directors meeting, someone suggested that perhaps these questions should be posed to leading pastors in Russia and Ukraine. After all, Peter and BIEM had established close relationships with many godly men who were strategically placed and able to provide answers from their point of view overseas. What would they recommend as the most effective strategy for BIEM?

When that question was posed, pastors in Russia and Ukraine responded unanimously. One pastor answered the question in a particularly vivid way. He explained, "Here in our country we are in the midst of a huge harvest. We have plenty of laborers. Our young men are on fire for God and ready to preach the Gospel and reach their people. What we need most of all, are sickles for the harvest." This pastor went on to explain that their greatest need was theological training, support and equipping of their own people to plant churches. Other Russian and Ukrainian pastors echoed this response, which resonated with Peter and all at BIEM who always felt that the most effective missionary work was that which focused on planting local churches.

Therefore Peter and BIEM transitioned to a focus on planting churches by supporting, training, and equipping nationals, so this activity became the third phase of BIEM's ministry.

However, while it is a simple decision to alter the course of a mission agency in leadership meetings at the mission's headquarters, no one assumed that BIEM's constituency of supporting pastors, churches, and individuals would understand and welcome the new direction. Peter and Sam embraced every opportunity to discuss and explain the new course into which God had led BIEM. In a 1992 article entitled "National Church Planters & Missionaries," Peter offered the following information as he explained the opportunity and need for supporting and equipping national church planters:

> It often takes several years and over $250,000 for an American missionary to raise his support, move to the

field, learn the language, and adapt to the culture. There is, doubtless, a need for American missionaries in Russia and Ukraine, where they are certain to play an important role. However, wise stewardship and economic reality encourage us to undertake the support of national missionaries as well in that unique and newly open field. While this policy has its detractors and its problems, we feel that its potential justifies our efforts to equip, train, and support nationals.

Russia and the other CIS [i.e., Commonwealth of Independent States, a loose association of some countries that were formerly part of the Soviet Union] nations have an available pool of zealous, committed, called, and willing workers. They already know the language and culture. In many cases they have been tried and proven by persecution and suffering. Should the doors to their countries close, they could remain in place. Supporting such men is a great way to invest missionary funds.

Following are excerpts from an article in the *Challenger* that also developed reasons for the new emphasis.

Sickles for the Harvest: Training and Equipping Russian National Christians

By Missionary Sam Slobodian

Many people are responding to the Gospel as a result of evangelistic effort and an awakening of spiritual interest among Russian people. However, because of the lack of trained servants of God, not many people are being discipled. Surveying sources both within and without the former Soviet Union, we believe it is quite clear that the greatest need is the need to train and equip leaders.

A vast majority of the new converts in Russia are under thirty, and many of the new Christians are public school teachers and other professionals with higher education. This development is exciting because such people could be excellent prospects to assume leadership positions in the future. However, Christians in the former Soviet bloc are not able to engage in conversation with their highly educated countrymen and do not have answers to the kinds of questions asked by intellectuals.

Throughout the repressive history of the Soviet Union theological education and other ministry training was severely curtailed by the government. Lenin launched the first attack on religious instruction in 1918 by outlawing religious teaching in public and private schools. Religious training could only be given in seminaries where students were permitted to study only theology, and very few seminaries were given the special permission required by the government, which closed thousands of churches and most religious schools. In the decades that followed, formal theological education all but disappeared with only a handful of Russian Orthodox seminaries staying open with a minuscule number of students.

Tragically, accompanying the closure and repression of these schools was the persecution, imprisonment, and the even martyrdom of many pastors and Christian leaders. While decades of anti-religious indoctrination, repression, and persecution did not destroy the Christian faith as the government hoped, it did result in generations of Christians who lacked theological education and ministry training.

As evangelical leaders and missiologists evaluate the need for theological education in Eastern Europe today, many would agree with the assessment of Helmuth Egelkraut of the European Evangelical Accrediting Association, when he finds Russia to be the most underdeveloped among the

Eastern European community in terms of theological education and leadership training. In Russia the situation seems to be the worst, with many congregations having no trained leaders.

We have found the situation among the Baptist churches with which BIEM works to be in similar need. For many generations Baptists were simply not allowed to have access to higher education. When one fellowships with Baptists in Russia, Ukraine, and other CIS countries today, it is quite normal to hear the testimony of many who were expelled or forced out of universities and technical schools after their faith was revealed. While it is certainly true that Christians outside the Baptist faith endured similar treatment, the Bourdeaux's (Lorena and Michael), who have long been regarded as leading authorities on the persecuted church under Communism, note the following:

The continuing low educational level of Soviet Baptists is attributable not merely to the appeal of the movement to workers, as may appear on the surface, though this is certainly part of the truth. There is also systematic prohibition of higher education for Christian teenagers; they are inevitably assigned to menial jobs. For many years the Baptist church was unable even minimally to compensate by providing theological education for its own leaders, a privilege which had been extended to the Russian Orthodox Church immediately after World War II.

Compounding the difficulty of this situation was the scarcity of books and written materials for theological and pastoral study. Most pastors in Russia counted themselves fortunate to have a Bible. Christian books were routinely confiscated as "anti-government propaganda," and those in possession of such materials were regarded and treated like criminals. To a large extent, the Soviet Christians had no Bible dictionaries, concordances, or other resources to help them with their studies. As a result, their knowledge of doctrine and theology was very limited....

These problems can largely be traced to a leadership vacuum in both quantity and quality.

The need for training leaders has been seen and spoken to by Christian leaders from within the former Soviet Union itself. A 12-member international listening team assembled 40 Christian leaders from within the former Soviet Union and Soviet bloc countries and compiled reports and made recommendations to Western missions based on the leaders' meetings. One of their conclusions was since "churches in the former eastern bloc are hindered by lack of trained leadership and decades of isolation from the mainstream of society," Western missions should "spend less time speaking in Sunday worship services, and more time teaching and equipping young leaders."

I heard the need explained by a Russian Christian in this way, "We are in the midst of a great harvest, and we have an abundance of laborers. But alas, we have not enough sickles." The imagery is clear and powerful. There is a great harvest to be had for our Lord in the rich harvest fields of Russia today, and there is an available force of dedicated laborers to reap it. But they need tools (sickles) to do the work. The tools which need to be provided are theological studies, pastoral and leadership training, and books, as well as other materials which will equip them for the fields.

(*Baptist International Challenger*, Vol. 12, No.3, 1994)

Thus, in 1991 BIEM began supporting national missionaries. An interesting observation is that the evangelistic campaigns which characterized the second phase of BIEM's ministry dovetailed neatly with the planting of churches by national missionaries, which emerged as the third phase of BIEM's outreach. Evangelistic campaigns were organized in communities that were targeted for new churches, which would be planted by BIEM national missionaries. These evangelistic services, which featured Peter Slobodian's preaching, played a key

Peter and Sam, meeting with some of BIEM's first national church planters.

role in the foundation for the new works. God greatly blessed Peter's preaching, and a multitude of souls repented of sin and accepted Christ as Savior in these meetings. National church planters were in place to work with the newly saved converts, who became the nucleus of newly established churches.

Meanwhile, back in Chicago a special celebration was brewing for Peter. Even though his sights were often focused on Eastern Europe by that time, the souls he had won to Christ in Chicago remembered that he had a special birthday approaching. The date July 10, 1993, became an unforgettable day for Peter Slobodian because it was on that day that friends and family gathered at the *Primera Iglesia Bautista Fundamental* (First Fundamental Baptist Church) to celebrate Peter's seventieth birthday and his fiftieth year of preaching the Gospel. (Those figures were particularly remarkable because since Peter

The Lewshenias came to celebrate Peter's 50 years of ministry.

often jokingly claimed that he was only thirty-five. Reflecting the humor, one of the deacons declared that he finally understood how he could have thirty-five years under his belt. "Pastor," he said, "You have thirty-five years on your left leg, and thirty-five years on your right leg.")

The highlight on that joyful day of festivities was the surprise appearance of Constantine and Elizabeth Lewshenia. Peter was both totally flabbergasted and delighted to see once again the missionary who had led him to Christ so many decades earlier. Though officially retired in 1990 after fifty years of ministry with SGA, the Lewshenias were still actively serving the Lord, and Constantine had just recently returned from his fourth preaching and teaching trip to Russia and Ukraine. The reunion of these remarkable servants of God on that occasion was a sweet and cherished experience.

Back to Russia

In 1994, the city of Volokalamsk west of Moscow was targeted for a new work. A BIEM national missionary made arrangements to

Peter preaching inside the theater in Volokalamsk, Russia. A church was later started nearby.

conduct evangelistic meetings in a local cinema. The national missionary promoted the evangelistic meetings, which took place in the spring of 1994 when Peter and Sam arrived with Dr. David Tessman and Pastor Greg Wahlberg from the United States. Over one hundred people came to Christ during three days of meetings. As the national missionary continued to work with the converts and contacts from the evangelistic campaign, a solid new church developed. Following are excerpts from David Tessman's journal concerning that event:

Excerpts from "A Missions Trip to Russia: April 27 – May 11, 1994"

by Dr. David Tessmann

Friday, May 6

...The Russian Orthodox church in Volokolamsk was actually working to oppose the meetings. The local paper carried an advertisement of the meetings. The Orthodox priest asked the newspaper editor who gave him permission to advertise the meetings? He replied, "And who gave you the permission to ask me?" An electrical engineer from the Baptist church at Dyedovsk has a real burden for the city and has been going there the last few months. He has seen some souls saved.... We had noon lunch with three of these new converts. These ladies were in their upper 50's, and their faces glowed with a love and excitement for Christ. They placed 26 large posters in public places in the city and distributed many announcements in mailboxes of the people. A 300-seat

Peter standing beside one of the posters announcing the evangelistic services.

auditorium was rented in the city. The first meeting saw 122 visitors, with 41 responding to the gospel invitation.

Saturday, May 7 (Kiev)

When we arrived at the church five minutes before the conference began, we noticed only one car. Inside the build-

Pastor Tessman, Pastor Wahlberg, and Peter and Sam with Pastor Nikolai Velichko.

ing were 91 Ukrainian pastors and deacons, many who traveled all night by train. Most pastors do not own their own cars. Many carried suitcases. The three and a half hour lecture on cults began and was well received. We did not have enough books for all. The pastors ran to the front grabbing to get a book. After a delicious lunch prepared by the host church, but paid for by BIEM, the second lecture on the charismatic movement was held. The pastors stood for two hours afterward with many questions....

At midnight Sam called to inform us of 64 saved at the second meeting on Sunday at Volokolamsk.... At the third meeting in Volokolamsk 154 attended. There were 70 professions of faith. A sound system was obtained which greatly helped the service.

Sunday, May 8

The final meeting in Volokolamsk took place that evening. The auditorium was nearly full. Estimates were that there were some 200 in attendance for a great service, which included the church choir from Dyedovsk. Sam Slobodian played his trumpet, and special musical was presented by about 25 children who earned a children's Bible by their faithful attendance. Many parents came to see this presentation. After Peter Slobodian preached a message on Nicodemus, 73 trusted Christ.

Afterward there was a wonderful time of food and fellowship in one of the church workers' home. All rejoiced in the great boost this young church received from these meetings. When the church was started by the BIEM national missionary about one year ago, there was only one elderly Christian lady in Volokolamsk. Now this young church was averaging 40 adults and 30 youth and are sure to have their numbers increase from this three-day campaign. The missionary pastor and people were grateful for God's great hand of blessing on these meetings. Prayer is needed for this young church, new converts, and national missionary as they have much follow-up work to do.

(Personal journal entries used by permission of Pastor David Tessman)

A New Use for an Old Building

The city of Dyedovsk on the outskirts of Moscow is another example of a community where evangelistic meetings played an important role in planting a church. Dyedovsk was home to the church that was pastored by Peter Rumachik, who once served as the vice president of the large group of unregistered Baptist churches that were so severely persecuted for the faith.

Pastor Rumachik himself was particularly singled out for harsh treatment by Soviet authorities, and as a result he ended up spending over eighteen years in Soviet prisons and labor camps.

Evangelistic campaigns were organized in the city's local cultural center, or literally, the "House of Culture." This was the exact same

Evangelistic meeting held outside the cultural center in Dyedovsk, Russia.

building in which Peter Rumachik had been publicly put on trial along with four other church members in a highly publicized trial that was described in the press as a day when cultists who engaged in child-sacrifice and other heinous crimes would be tried and sentenced. Back at that time, such a large, angry mob gathered that police had to call for reinforcements to rush Peter and the other Christians being tried into the auditorium for their trial. There, in front of a hostile, jeering audience, each of the defendants received a long prison term.

Now, years later, Christians were holding public evangelistic meetings in that *very same* auditorium. Peter Rumachik and Peter Slobodian and others were able to preach God's word without opposition. Not only were hundreds saved, but the new church that was born through those evangelistic services continued to meet in that very same House of Culture for years. Eventually the congregation relocated to a new building in town. Pastor Peter Rumachik had often been mentioned in BIEM's *Challenger*, which publicized the plight of persecuted Christians. Now he and BIEM forged a strong relationship, and many of BIEM's early Russian church planters came from Pastor Rumachik's church—including his own son Pavel Rumachik.

BIEM's first church-planting efforts were in the Moscow area. Later St. Petersburg was included, as well as the Volga River area and Tulskaya Oblast. One of BIEM's missionaries went to Magadan, which is on the Sea of Okhotsk (northwest of Japan) in the Far East of Russia.

Peter and Sam with the Rumachiks and church planting couples.

In Ukraine, church-planting efforts began in the capital city of Kiev, then spread to surrounding areas and eventually extended to Lutsk and Ternopil in Western Ukraine. Moldova, Romania, Georgia, and Belarus were added as BIEM expanded its work in those nearby countries by employing the same strategy of planting churches by training and supporting nationals.

A key matter that had to be addressed as Peter and BIEM were launching these church-planting efforts was the training of the nation-

Peter meeting with the Brotherhood of Independent Baptist Churches of Ukraine.

als who would serve as missionaries, pastors and in other ministry positions. BIEM didn't have sufficient personnel in place to undertake such a massive effort. The solution was to recruit pastors and professors from Bible colleges or seminaries to travel overseas to teach modular sessions, which turned out to be a very practical solution. At first, seminars which were conducted so that men could receive basic theological training. Eventually schools were established. In 1994, the Brotherhood of Independent Baptist Churches of Ukraine established Kiev Theological Baptist Seminary in partnership with BIEM and Dr. Peter Slobodian, who served as President of the School. Later, a similar school was established near Moscow in conjunction with an association of independent Baptist churches, several of which had been started by BIEM national church planters. Eventually BIEM missionaries and directors established modular schools in Romania and Moldova as well.

As these schools produced graduates, many of whom went on to establish new churches, BIEM's outreach expanded significantly, all of which was a cause of great delight to Peter. After all these decades

Peter Slobodian with students and teachers of Kiev Theological Seminary.

in the Western Hemisphere, his dream of evangelizing in Eastern Europe and beyond was coming true. God was certainly blessing!

In 2001 BIEM celebrated twenty years of ministry with a conference near Moscow. As BIEM's founder, Peter was the featured speaker at this event, which was attended by BIEM missionaries and partners from several nations. The conference was a special milestone for Peter, since God enabled him to see his vision realized as BIEM had expanded to become a significant force for missions in Russia and Eastern Europe. Following are two articles from the *Challenger* that describe this conference:

BIEM's 20-Year Anniversary Conference Makes History

After months of anticipation and planning, BIEM celebrated 20 years of ministry at Rumyantsevo Christian Camp on the outskirts of Moscow. Over 100 national pastors and Christian workers came from Russia, Moldova, Ukraine and Romania for this historic event. A delegation from the United States brought the total number of registered guests to 120. Since an impressive crew of cooks, servers and other workers were needed to conduct the conference, the entire number of participants filled the camp to its 150-person capacity.

One would probably think that the delegation from America made the longest journey to get to the conference. Not so. The prize for the most arduous journey goes to those who came from Magadan, Russia, the ministry site of BIEM Missionary Tim Smith. So vast is the expanse of Russia that Magadan, north of the Sea of Japan, is located roughly the same distance from Moscow as Grand Rapids, Michigan. The journey required several hours of travel by plane and five days by train to cross the length of Siberia to get to Moscow.

The three-day event featured ministry reports from all the areas where BIEM is working. These informative sessions were held during the mornings and afternoons, and they proved to be a great blessing as BIEM workers were able to become acquainted with their counterparts in other countries. The evenings featured uplifting services with great preaching. One especially notable speaker during the conference was BIEM Founder Dr. Peter Slobodian, whose passion for the Word of God burned just as clearly when he opened the conference on Thursday, October 4, as it did when he was preaching by shortwave radio into the Soviet Union. Other speakers included two former prisoners for the Faith: Pastor Peter Rumachik, who served as vice president of the large group of unregistered Baptist Churches and Nikolai Velichko, who is the president of the Brotherhood of Independent Baptist Churches of Ukraine.

On Friday morning, the conference got into full swing with a report from BIEM President Dr. Sam Slobodian, who gave an outline of the current ministries of the Mission, which has expanded into four countries where BIEM has planted 40 churches and is training over 200 nationals.

Peter Slobodian preaching at BIEM's 20th anniversary conference.

The reports of Friday morning highlighted the efforts in the Moscow area, where BIEM missionaries have planted over one dozen churches. A special highlight in the ministry reports from the Moscow area was the report on the drug rehabilitation center started by BIEM church planter Pavel Rumachik. One of the American delegates stated after seeing the presentation, "I was impressed, because this wasn't just some 12-step program, but the Word of God affecting the hearts of men."

As the reports continued, delegates shared how the Word of God had affected the hearts of men through church planting efforts in the St. Petersburg area. Though many report that this area has grown very cold to the gospel, the Lord continues to bless the ministries there with receptive hearts. Much is being done with orphans and homeless children, who are being clothed and fed as they are taught the transforming Word of God.

Peter with Eugene Buyko, who became BIEM's director for Ukraine.

Half of Friday afternoon was dedicated to reports from Ukraine, where the biggest obstacle to new ministry seems to be only that not enough laborers are available to reap the harvest. In recent months, a multitude of new areas have been opened to the gospel, and BIEM's Kyiv school continues to produce much-needed graduates, whose training has enabled several to start new church planting efforts in various cities. The rest of the afternoon featured accounts of the work in Moldova and Romania by national missionaries and by the BIEM mission director for those areas, Fred Canaday.

On Saturday, BIEM Missionary Tim Smith began the session with a report on ministering with the Chukchi People—an ethnic group similar to the Eskimos—in the Russian Far North. Dr. Ron Brewer, BIEM's director of educational programming, then went into a detailed account of the effective labors of the Mission to train nationals in Kyiv, the Moscow area, and Moldova. Pastor Aleksei

Smirnov closed the conference by detailing the special partnership between BIEM and the Association of Brotherly Churches, a fellowship of fully independent Baptist churches in Moscow Region.

Youth choir from Kiev.

Inspirational music played an important role in this conference as workers from the various republics ministered to each other with numbers from their own respective areas and languages. One key ingredient was the participation of the youth choir from Puhova Street Baptist Church in Kyiv; this group has often participated in evangelism and new church-planting efforts, and they were a blessing to all present.

Another highlight was music composed and sung by former drug addicts brought to Christ through the ministry in Nahabino. A special word of thanks should go to the interpreters. Without their tireless work of constantly translating into Russian, Ukrainian, Romanian and English, this conference would not have been possible.

This was truly a historic event, and the impact in hearts and lives was readily seen in the dedicated missionaries and workers of BIEM. Brother Stanislav, who had accompanied Missionary Tim Smith from Magadan, was called to preach. This was a great answer to prayer for Brother Smith and the many who support his ministry.

The warm fellowship brought home the theme verse to all in attendance: "For we are laborers together with God"

(1 Corinthians 3:9). Though most of you who make our ministry possible through your prayers and support couldn't

Peter Slobodian pictured with some of BIEM's church planters and missionaries who attended the 20th anniversary conference.

be there, you were well represented by the Americans who were able to come and by Brother Larry Schonert, who was selected by the American delegation to speak at the conference on behalf of the American supporters. Therefore, in the minds and hearts of all present, each of you involved in our ministry was recognized as a participant in this conference. Please accept the many heartfelt words of thanks and appreciation offered to you by many nationals and other workers during this joyous event. We are grateful for the privilege of being partners with you in the work that God is doing in Russia and Eastern Europe today.

(*Baptist International Challenger,* Vol. 20, No. 1, 2002)

Conference Highlights the Scope of BIEM's Ministry

BIEM's approach to fulfilling the missionary mandate in Russia and Eastern Europe features the support, training and equipping of dedicated and prepared nationals.

Through the partnership of our American prayer and support base with national Christians and churches, BIEM has been able to reach countless souls and plant many churches in Russia, Ukraine, Moldova and Romania.

BIEM's first church planting efforts concentrated in capital cities of Moscow, Russia, and Kyiv, Ukraine.

After establishing several churches in the Moscow region, BIEM national church planters began new works in Myshkin along the Volga River, and in Dubovka, which is in the Tula coal-mining area. A growing team of BIEM missionaries is now planting churches in the St. Petersburg area of Russia. Church planting efforts in Ukraine have expanded beyond the Kyiv area to several cities and villages in Central Ukraine. This year BIEM plans to branch out into Western Ukraine through a church planting effort in Lutsk.

Church planting ministries in Moldova grew like the ministries in Russia and Ukraine. After first planting a strong church in the capital city, a faithful team of BIEM missionaries is now effectively reaching towns and villages in the outlying areas. BIEM church planting efforts in Romania which began in the Oradea area have now expanded to Fetesti and the surrounding areas. Plans are underway for starting new churches in several needy locations there.

Thus far, these efforts have resulted in planting 40 churches since 1992. One dozen of these churches are now self-supporting, and several have been able to build or obtain their own buildings. The greatest missionary need in this part of the world may well be the training of nationals. BIEM personnel are currently training over 200 nationals in five different locations in Eastern Europe.

(*Baptist International Challenger,* Vol. 20, No. 1, 2002)

Closing note on Peter Slobodian

Before moving to America, while Peter still labored as a missionary in South America, he was receiving monthly financial support through a mission agency. However, one time the mission didn't receive its support. So the General Director wrote a letter to the missionaries and explained that there would be a delay before the mission could pay them. In the meantime, he advised that every missionary should try to find some sort of temporary work to support themselves until funds could be forwarded as usual.

Suddenly Peter found himself needing a job. Because he knew how to farm, he searched for an opening where he could perform farm work, but couldn't find anyone hiring. Then Peter remembered that his grandfather on his mother's side had been a wealthy farmer and businessman. Farming was extremely strenuous manual labor, but running a business required more brains than muscle.

So, following his grandfather's example, Peter decided that he would become a businessman. After all, Peter had already graduated from business school before applying to the Bible institute. Combining his faith with his work, Peter started selling Bibles, New Testaments, and other literature in various provinces. Selling Bibles proved to be very successful, and it gave Peter and Mary a decent income. In addition, being a Bible salesman gave opportunities to witness to people about the Lord. This temporary business also opened doors to conduct evangelistic campaigns in which many people gave their hearts to Christ. In some places, new churches were established as a result of these campaigns.

In addition to the revenues that Peter earned from selling Bibles, New Testaments, and other literature in various languages, Mary provided another source of income. Being quite artistic, she painted oil pictures and Bible verses on glass and canvas. Peter ordered glass and art supplies, and he constructed frames for her creations. People from various provinces purchased her artwork. The combination of Peter's and Mary's efforts provided good money—so good that friends in South America were surprised that they planned to leave for North

America. They said, “You don’t have to go to the United States. You’re doing fine right here.”

“We don’t want to go to the United States because of money, but with the goal of studying and praising the Lord.”

Years later, near the end of his earthly life, Peter reflected on those days and on his decision to study in America. “God helped us to accomplish our purpose,” he said. “He opened a great door. He enabled us to get an education, and we used that education for Him.”

Peter Slobodian beside his display
at a missions conference.

Now, looking back on all this history, one can only marvel at how mightily the Lord used this man who grew up in a poor family in an obscure village in Western Ukraine. But what if he had passed up opportunities to receiving training in the Word of God? Or what if he had been satisfied to remain in Argentina and to earn a comfortable living selling Bibles and homemade artwork? It’s literally impossible to guess how many lives Peter Slobodian touched through evangelizing, by church planting in the U.S., by preaching over radio waves that crisscrossed the globe and were possibly were heard by millions of people, and by establishing Bible schools that would train up younger generations of dedicated believers to go out and join in the spiritual harvest. But, praise God, Peter and Mary Slobodian’s vision wasn’t fixed on earthly rewards, but rather on heavenly goals. Indeed, Peter was constantly “Looking unto Jesus the author and finisher of our faith; who for the joy that was set before him endured the cross, despising the shame, and is set down at the right hand of the throne of God” (Hebrews 12:2).

Peter Passes into Eternity

Right to the end of his earthly days, even as his strength was ebbing, Peter Slobodian hoped for one last chance to visit the land where he was born so that he could preach God's Good News of salvation there. However, as his health deteriorated and he had to make repeated visits to the hospital, it became clear that another trans-Atlantic crossing was simply out of the question. Instead, Peter prepared his heart for a much more important, long-awaited journey—the trip into eternity to meet face to face the Lord whom he had preached about for so many years.

Here is the article that announced Peter's home-going in BIEM's *Challenger* newsletter (Vol. 23, No. 3, 2005):

BIEM's Founder with the Lord

On June 24, 2005, a special warrior for the Faith went to the Savior to receive his heavenly reward. On that date, BIEM's founder—Peter Antonovich Slobodian—finally stood in the presence of the Lord he had served most of his life.

BIEM's Founder, Dr. Peter Slobodian, went to be with his Lord on June 24, 2005.

Although not all of BIEM's supporters knew Peter personally, even those who didn't will appreciate what a rich and varied life this servant of God led.

Early life

Born on July 9, 1923, in the village of Hlibiv, Ukraine, Peter was raised by a Greek Catholic father, who was

Ukrainian, and a Roman Catholic mother, who was Polish. However, Peter's father lost his faith in his church when a cat knocked over and broke a statue of the Virgin Mary. "How can that statue help us if it could not even save itself?" he said.

Because life in Ukraine was a struggle, Anton Slobodian decided to sail to Argentina and find work. However, earning money in Argentina also proved difficult. After six long years he was finally able to arrange for his wife and children to join him in South America. Before they arrived, Anton had read a Ukrainian New Testament, came to a true understanding of salvation by grace, and put his trust in Christ as Savior.

Unfortunately, by this time Peter had already turned 12, which required an adult fare, so there wasn't enough money for the whole family to join Anton. As a result, Peter remained in Ukraine. Two years later, at the age of 14, he traveled alone from Ukraine to Argentina by cargo ship.

Born again

Working alongside his father, young Peter learned how difficult farming can be. So when he was grown, he went to Buenos Aires to study business. He had no interest in church or God.

One day Peter wanted to go to a dance, but his friend was curious about an American missionary named Constantine Lewshenia, and wanted to go hear him.

"All right," Peter consented. "Let's go. But if I don't like it, I'll go to the dance by myself, and you can stay in church." Peter ended up staying.

The next night Peter returned to hear the missionary one last time. As he later said, "Listening to his preaching, I realized that I was looking for some kind of peace, and I couldn't find it. Then I realized that I couldn't get it because

I was looking in all the wrong places." That night Peter repented of his sins and accepted Christ as his personal Savior.

This happened just two weeks before Peter graduated with a degree in business. Instead of becoming a businessman, Peter felt God's call to become something else—a preacher of the Gospel. He applied to the Russian Bible Institute in Rosario, Argentina, and graduated at the top of his class.

Laboring for the Lord

In addition to founding a Slavic Baptist church for immigrants, Peter traveled to other provinces and even to Paraguay and Brazil to evangelize. He married Mary Ermacovitch, whom he met at the Bible institute

Through Peter and Mary's friendships with missionaries, they learned about opportunities for higher Christian education in the United States. So they traveled to the U.S. to study.

In Minneapolis Peter found thousands of immigrants from Eastern Europe listed in the telephone book. Even as students, he and Mary visited these people at their homes to witness. Next he began holding home Bible studies. From these was born yet another Slavic Baptist church in Minneapolis, plus a Ukrainian Baptist church. Such ministries required Peter to preach in various languages, including Spanish, English, Russian, and Ukrainian. Because of this, one rumor stated

Peter and Mary Slobodian.

that if Peter found an unbeliever he couldn't understand, he would go away and study that person's language and then return to share the Gospel!

After graduating from Bible college (he eventually earned two masters degrees and two doctorates), Peter yearned to be a missionary to the Soviet Union, but that dream wasn't possible in those days. Instead the couple moved to Chicago and became missionaries to the thousands of immigrants from Eastern Europe and the Spanish-speaking world.

As time passed, however, the urge in Peter's heart to preach to lost souls in his original homeland grew. So in 1981 Peter founded Baptist International Evangelistic Ministries to broadcast Gospel messages to the Soviet Union by shortwave radio. Later, when openness came to those lands, he was able to travel back to the USSR for the first time in decades. He even revisited the village of Hlibiv, where he was born.

By the time the Soviet Union collapsed, BIEM had forged strong ties with churches in Russia and Eastern Europe. By 1992 actual church planting had replaced radio work as the core ministry.

In his eighties, despite failing strength, Peter Slobodian often talked about possibly traveling to Russia one last time. Instead, the Lord gave him a trip that was even more precious—the journey to his heavenly home.

As 2 Timothy 4:7 says of the Apostle Paul, Peter Slobodian likewise fought a good fight, he finished his course, he kept the faith.

Appendix

A Sermon by Peter Slobodian

Peter Slobodian preached a huge percentage of his sermons in languages other than English. The following message, titled "Ye Must Be Born Again," is one of those that was broadcast multiple times from international shortwave stations. For readers of English, this sermon has been translated below from the Russian language. This and other audio sermons by Peter Slobodian are accessible on the website of Baptist International Evangelistic Ministries.

Ye Must Be Born Again

And now we will read from the Holy Scriptures, the Gospel of John, chapter 3, verses 1 through 5. We read here the following words:

> *"There was a man of the Pharisees, named Nicodemus, a ruler of the Jews: The same came to Jesus by night, and said unto him, Rabbi, we know that thou art a teacher come from God: for no man can do these miracles that thou doest, except God be with him. Jesus answered and said unto him, Verily, verily, I say unto thee, Except a man be born again, he cannot see the kingdom of God. Nicodemus saith unto him, How can a man be born when he is old? can he enter the second time into his mother's womb, and be born? Jesus answered, Verily, verily, I say unto thee, Except a man be born of water and of the Spirit, he cannot enter into the kingdom of God."*

Let's pray. Our heavenly Father, we come to You in the name of Jesus Christ. We thank You for Your Word and ask You, Lord, that You would talk to the hearts of those who are not born again yet, that they would receive Christ. Hear us, we ask You in the name of our Savior Jesus Christ. Amen.

My topic is, "How to Be Born Again." The passage of Scripture we have read teaches us that it is necessary to be born again to see or to enter into the kingdom of God.

Here we have the story of Nicodemus, who came to Jesus at night. He was a highly educated man, very religious, and also had an important religious position. Since he was a Pharisee, a ruler of the Jews and a teacher of Israel, he did not want people to see him with Christ. Therefore, he came to Him at night. Being held in respect and honor himself, he honored Christ with the title of a teacher. He also mentioned that Jesus is a teacher come from God. At the same time, he testified about miracles that Christ had performed. Christ listened to Nicodemus and, being aware of his great need as a sinner, told him, *"Verily, verily, I say unto thee, except a man be born again, he cannot see the kingdom of God."*

Dear friends, the issue of being born again is a very important one. Where you will spend your eternal destiny is determined by your decision on this matter. Since being born again determines the eternal destiny of the sinner, then what does it mean to be born again?

Being born again does not mean a changing of the old nature, as some people think. To change one's old nature and lay aside bad habits and vices is a very good thing to do, but it is not the same as being born again. Neither does being born again mean reformation. Reformation is a good thing, but it is still not the same as being born again.

Being born again also does not mean to be baptized, as many teach. Hell will be filled with baptized people who have not been born again. Baptism is important, and the Holy Scriptures teach about baptism clearly and with great detail. However, it is not the same as being born again.

Furthermore, being born again does not mean heritage from parents. Many think that if the parents have been born again, then their children can naturally inherit this blessing. No, dear friends! Nobody can inherit being born again. We can only experience it personally.

Now, if to be born again does not mean changing of the old nature, does not mean reformation, does not mean baptism, and does not mean heritage from parents, then what does it mean to be born again? On the authority of the Holy Scripture, to be born again is a work of the Holy Spirit! Jesus Christ stated and explained this clearly to Nicodemus, as it is written in verse 6:

> *"Verily, verily, I say unto thee, Except a man be born of water and of the Spirit, he cannot enter into the kingdom of God."*

Christ said, "*Of water and of the Spirit.*" Water, according to the teaching of Christ, represents the Holy Spirit. We read in the Gospel of John, chapter 7, verses 37–39, the following words:

> *In the last day, that great day of the feast, Jesus stood and cried, saying, If any man thirst, let him come unto me, and drink. He that believeth on me, as the scripture hath said, out of his belly shall flow rivers of living water. But this spake he of the Spirit, which they that believe on him should receive….*

In other words it may be said that to be born again means being born from God. We read about this in the Gospel of John, chapter 1, verses 12–13 where the following is said:

> *But as many as received him, to them gave he power to become the sons of God, even to them that believe on his name: Which were born, not of blood, nor of the will of the flesh, nor of the will of man, but of God.*

Being born again also involves the quickening, or life-giving, to a dead being. You may ask,

"How you can say that this or that man is dead? This man moves, he walks, he works, doesn't he? And you say that he is dead?"

Yes, dear friends! On the basis of the Holy Scripture, a man without Christ is dead. He is dead by his transgressions and sins. In Ephesians chapter 2, verses 1–5, we read the following words:

And you hath he quickened, who were dead in trespasses and sins; wherein in time past ye walked according to the course of this world, according to the prince of the power of the air, the spirit that now worketh in the children of disobedience: Among whom also we all had our conversation in times past in the lusts of our flesh, fulfilling the desires of the flesh and of the mind; and were by nature the children of wrath, even as others. But God, who is rich in mercy, for his great love wherewith he loved us, Even when we were dead in sins, hath quickened us together with Christ, by grace ye are saved....

Once, two men were walking in the woods, and they saw a turtle. One of them said, "This turtle is dead." The other man disagreed and said, "No, this turtle is alive." Wanting to prove that the turtle was alive, the second man added, "This turtle is alive because it is moving." Hearing those words, his friend objected and said, "The turtle doesn't know that it is dead; that is why it is still moving."

Indeed, dear friends, poor sinners do not know that they are dead, and so they are still moving! We have a good Biblical example of this written in the Gospel of Luke, Chapter 15, where Christ tells about the younger son who told to his father, "*Father, give me the portion of goods that falleth to me.*" The younger son wanted to prove that he can live and do what he wants to do and in the way he wants to do it.

The father divided unto them his living. And not many days after the younger son gathered all together, and took his journey into a far country, and there wasted his substance with riotous living. And when he had spent all, there arose a mighty famine in that land; and he began to be in want. And he went and joined himself to a citizen of that country; and he sent him into his fields to feed swine. And he would fain have filled his belly with the husks that the swine did eat: and no man gave unto him. And when he came to himself, he said, How many hired servants of my father's have bread enough and to spare, and I perish with hunger! I will arise and go to my father, and will say unto him, Father, I have sinned against heaven, and before thee, And am no more worthy to be called thy son: make me as one of thy hired servants.

This young man did not just make a decision as many people do who say things yet never act on them. He stood up and went to his father.

The father probably many times thought of and waited for his son, saying in his heart: "Maybe my younger son will come to himself and come back." One day, he was looking out and saw that somebody was coming. It probably was impossible to recognize the son from a distance since both his clothes and his shoes were worn out and ragged. He was tired and tormented by sin.

But when he was yet a great way off, his father saw him, and had compassion, and ran, and fell on his neck, and kissed him. And the son said unto him, Father, I have sinned against heaven, and in thy sight, and am no more worthy to be called thy son. But the father said to his servants, Bring forth the best robe, and put it on him; and put a ring on his hand, and shoes on his feet: And bring hither the fatted calf, and kill it; and let us eat, and be merry: For this my son was dead, and is alive again; he was lost, and is found. And they began to be merry.

This is exactly what is means to be born again. It is a quickening, or giving life to a dead being. Come back to the heavenly Father! *"For this my son was dead, and is alive again,"* said the father.

Furthermore, being born again also means becoming a new creature. Paul the Apostle says in 2 Corinthians, chapter 5 verse 17:

Therefore if any man be in Christ, he is a new creature: old things are passed away; behold, all things are become new.

The new robe is the righteousness of Christ. The new shoes are to go and preach the Gospel. The ring is that new and unbroken fellowship with the Lord. New friends, new hope, new joy, and a new song—everything is new! When a sinner is born again, he becomes a new creature. Since such a big change takes place in the life of a sinner after he is born again, many wonder, "How can a man be born again?"

Nicodemus asked Christ, *"How can a man be born when he is old?"* Being born again is from the Word of God. In James, chapter 1 verse 18, we read the following:

> *Of his own will begat he us with the word of truth, that we should be a kind of firstfruits of his creatures.*

James writes that He begot us with the word of truth. Christ told about this word of truth, which is the Holy Scripture, in His high priestly prayer in the Gospel of John, chapter 17 verse 17:

> *Sanctify them through thy truth: thy word is truth.*

Peter the Apostle also talks about this issue in 1 Peter, chapter 1 verse 23:

> *Being born again, not of corruptible seed, but of incorruptible, by the word of God, which liveth and abideth for ever.*

Being born again is from the Holy Spirit. Christ says, "*Verily, verily, I say unto thee, Except a man be born of water and of the Spirit, he cannot enter into the kingdom of God.*"

The second birth happens in a supernatural way. In the Gospel of John, chapter 3 verse 8 it is said:

> *The wind bloweth where it listeth, and thou hearest the sound thereof, but canst not tell whence it cometh, and whither it goeth: so is every one that is born of the Spirit.*

In the original text it is written that *the wind bloweth where it listeth.* One may say: "I do not see the wind therefore I do not believe that the wind exists." Yes, indeed, we cannot see the wind, but we can see the action of the wind. Not only can't we see the wind, but we also cannot taste the wind. Is it salty? Is it bitter? Or is it sweet? And not only these things, but if we would like to learn the weight of the wind, we would not be able to weigh the wind on any scales to learn its heaviness. But we see the action of the wind. "*The wind bloweth where it listeth*"—says Christ—"*So is every one that is born of the Spirit.*"

The work that we see is that which the Holy Spirit does in the life of a sinner. He makes him a son of God.

Does everybody need to be born again? Or just some people? Some think that only thieves, drinkers, robbers, and those who lead an immoral lifestyle need to be born again. Those who think this way try to express that there is no need in being born again for those who try to live a moral life, or those who are more educated, or those who lead a religious life. However, on the basis of the Holy Scripture, everybody needs to be born again.

Take Nicodemus, for example. He was a special person since he was a Pharisee, a ruler of the Jews and a teacher of Israel. If he, in order to see or enter the kingdom of God, had to be born again, then it clearly points out that everyone in the nation of Israel had to be born again to enter the kingdom of God. And if everyone in the nation of Israel had to be born again, that is, if the nation to whom God talked and to whom He gave His law, His promises, and His ministry had to be born again to enter the kingdom of God, then it is pure evidence that all human kind without any differentiation needs to be and must be born again.

Why is it necessary to be born again? It is necessary because the natural birth we have of flesh is flesh. Christ in the Gospel of John, chapter 3 verse 6, said:

> *That which is born of the flesh is flesh; and that which is born of the Spirit is spirit.*

Consider the time before the flood that is written about in Genesis chapter 6, when the wickedness of man was great in the earth and that every imagination of the thoughts of his heart was only evil continually. That is why God decided to destroy that world by a flood. In verse 3 it is said:

> *And the Lord said, My spirit shall not always strive with man, for that he also is flesh....*

Therefore, a human being needs to be born again. Furthermore, we also need to be born again because man who is flesh cannot please God. In Romans, chapter 8, verses 7–8 it is said:

> *Because the carnal mind is enmity against God: for it is not subject to the law of God, neither indeed can be. So then they that are in the flesh cannot please God.*

Isaiah the prophet in Chapter 64, verse 6 says:

> *But we are all as an unclean thing, and all our righteousnesses are as filthy rags....*

Paul the Apostle in Romans chapter 3, verse 10, states the sinful condition of both Jews and Gentiles in saying:

> *As it is written, There is none righteous, no, not one....*

And in verse 23 he proclaims:

> *For all have sinned, and come short of the glory of God....*

This is the proof of why it is necessary to be born again. Many ask what results from being born again? There is a remarkable result of being born again, because the born-again man is a child of God! It is said in the Gospel of John chapter 1, verse 12:

> *But as many as received him, to them gave he power to become the sons of God....*

Romans chapter 8 verses 14–16:

> *... the sons of God... have received the Spirit of adoption, whereby we cry, Abba, Father. The Spirit itself beareth witness with our spirit, that we are the children of God....*

Another result of being born again is that the born-again man worships God in spirit and truth. In the Gospel of John, chapter 4, verse 24, it is said:

> *God is a Spirit: and they that worship him must worship him in spirit and in truth.*

And not only that, but being born again results in a witness that such a one has eternal life. John the Apostle writes in 1 John chapter 5, verses 10–13:

> *He that believeth on the Son of God hath the witness in himself: he that believeth not God hath made him a liar; because he believeth not the record that God gave of his Son. And this is the record, that God hath given to us eternal life, and this life is in his Son. He that hath the Son hath life; and he that hath not the Son of God hath not life. These things have I written unto you that believe on the name of the Son of God; that ye may know that ye have eternal life, and that ye may believe on the name of the Son of God.*

Dear friends, are you born again? If not, you cannot see or enter the kingdom of God. Therefore, accept Jesus Christ right now, and you will become a new creature, a child of God! May God help you. Amen!

Let us pray. Our Heavenly Father, we thank You for Your Word. We ask You to talk to those hearts that have not received Christ, that they would accept Christ and be born again and receive the joy of serving You on Your field. Hear us in the name of Jesus Christ. Amen.

A Lasting Legacy

Along with a life full of souls saved and churches established, another lasting legacy left by the vision and efforts of Peter Slobodian is the mission BIEM, now led by his son Sam in the president's role.

Baptist International Evangelistic Ministries is an active and growing mission that emphasizes planting churches by training and supporting national workers dedicated to reaching their people for Christ.

Evangelism through missionary radio was the initial focus. BIEM's Gospel-preaching shortwave broadcasts in Russian and Ukrainian reached a Cold War audience of millions. Through Peter Slobodian's Gospel messages broadcast throughout the Soviet Union on several international short wave radio stations, countless souls came to Christ, and even churches were established through this "open door."

While missionary radio was the mission's main thrust in those days, BIEM also provided limited quantities of Bibles and material aid for believers under the yoke of communism. The mission published information about the plight of persecuted Christians, who were suffering for their faith. The Slobodians were occasionally able to travel to Communist lands, where they met with and gathered information from Christians living in the countries targeted by the radio broadcasts.

By the time the Soviet Union collapsed in the late 1980s, BIEM had established many strong relationships with pastors and churches in Russia and Eastern Europe. These relationships provided ideal contacts for recruiting, training, and supporting national church planters. In 1992, actual church planting became a reality as BIEM began to support and train national missionaries and workers. Soon, church planting replaced radio work as our core ministry, and new churches were established in Russia and Ukraine. In 1997, BIEM broadened its scope to include Romania and Moldova. Belarus and Georgia were eventually added, along with nations in Central and Western Asia. This expansion grew from a burden developed among BIEM missionaries and partners for the Muslim nations that were near Russia and Ukraine. More recently, BIEM began to support national missionaries

BIEM's 25th anniversary conference in Yalta, Ukraine.

in the Latin American countries of Peru and Ecuador. Additional facets of BIEM's church-planting program include distributing Bibles and Christian literature, evangelism, children's work, summer youth camps, and humanitarian aid.

While BIEM's American missionaries play vital roles in these outreaches, the mission's effective strategy places nationals in the forefront of ministry, minimizing the American presence as much as possible. In this productive partnership, nationals assume leadership roles in the churches being established, while American missionaries provide direction, training, accountability, and resources by serving as a link to an American support base interested in establishing indigenous churches.

Over 70 new churches have been established and over 40 building programs completed.

God has greatly blessed these efforts with over 70 new churches established and over 40 building programs undertaken. Many of these new churches have reached the goal of being 100% self-supporting. In turn, these new churches reach out to needy segments of society, which has expanded BIEM's influence into orphanages, public schools, hospitals, and military bases.

What are some advantages of BIEM's strategy?

An approach that emphasizes training nationals and helping them to establish their own churches with a minimum American presence provides a number of benefits:

- Nationals know their language and culture better than an American ever can.
- Modern politics can change quickly and radically. Even if a nation expels all American missionaries, our churches and programs can continue.
- Citizens of poorer nations often view Americans as "rich people." They can be jealous of America's prosperity. A strong American presence in new churches can create difficulties avoided by having national leadership.
- Building prices are kept to a minimum. Property owners overseas frequently jack up prices for land, buildings, and materials when selling to Americans. The Westerners have money, they think, so why not hold out for as much as possible? Letting local believers be in charge eliminates price games and stretches dollars for church building projects.

- Churches dependent on American leadership often struggle when turned over to national leadership. BIEM's strategy removes this transition process.

- It is cost-effective to use nationals whenever possible. Experts who study missions state that the combined costs of deputation, language classes, shipping personal belongings, acquiring housing on the foreign field, cost of living, etc., can reach as high as $250,000 to get one American onto a mission field.

- This strategy multiplies the effectiveness of Western missionaries. An American missionary can usually pastor only one church plant. However by training and equipping dedicated nationals, a missionary can establish many churches.

Okay, the strategy is effective. But is it Biblical?

Few people would doubt that the Apostle Paul was a successful church planter. How did he conduct his missionary work? Did Paul go to a new town, win souls, found a church—and then remain as pastor for many years?

No, he didn't. The Book of Acts recounts how Paul would travel to a spiritually needy area, witness, preach, teach, train, and then entrust the new congregation to a local man who had matured enough to accept the responsibility. Meanwhile, Paul would proceed to a new field to start this process afresh. When possible, he returned to see how the new churches were doing and reported back to sending churches. In fact, in Titus 1:5 Paul instructs Titus to operate in the same way.

Paul also engaged in administrative duties:

- He penned letters of instruction.
- He encouraged.
- He used assistants and messengers.
- He funneled offerings from believers in one land to needy believers in other lands.

Of course, this is not to say that American missionaries should not live on the foreign field. Some missionaries excel at hands-on, local work, and BIEM thanks God for sending us missions-minded Americans who live and labor overseas. Both American and national missionaries are needed. The point is, the strategy placing trained and equipped nationals in the forefront of ministry and administrating their efforts is both productive *and* Biblical.

How can churches in America help?

Take an interest in learning how the Gospel is going "even unto the end of the world" (Matthew 28:20).

Subscribe to our free *Challenger* newsletter, which shares current projects, victories, and prayer requests.

Consider contributing financial support (either regularly or a one-time gift) for a project, for one of our missionaries, or for BIEM's overall program. *(**Note:** In addition to raising funds for projects overseas, each of our U.S.-based directors must raise his own support for living and traveling expenses. BIEM is able to operate thanks to churches willing to consider them for missionary support.)*

Pray for us. No amount of human planning is a substitute for the power of prayer. We need God's wisdom and power on a daily basis.

Tell friends and family about our ministry. Maybe they would like to know what the Lord is doing in Russia and Eastern Europe, too!

For more information, contact:

Baptist International Evangelistic Ministries
P.O. Box 707
Danville, IN 46122-0707

Telephone: 317-718-1633
Email: missions@BaptistInternational.org
www.BaptistInternational.org